A HALF MILLION MILES
OF ROAD TRIPS

A HALF MILLION MILES OF ROAD TRIPS

Sam Allen

Route 66 MC Publications

Copyright © 2023 by Samuel N. Allen
All rights reserved

This book may not be reproduced in whole or in part or in any form or format without the written permission of the publisher.

Published by Route 66 MC Publications
100 Jackson St. Suite 305
Houston, Texas 77002

Manufactured in the United States of America

ISBN:
979-8-9885624-3-6 (color hardcover)
978-0-9904932-8-0 (color paperback)
979-8-9885624-0-5 (black and white paperback)
979-8-9885624-1-2 (ebook)

First Edition

Library of Congress Cataloging-in-Publication Data
Allen, Samuel N., 1955-
A Half Million Miles of Road Trips / Sam Allen

Cover design by Brian Love

Book interior and ebook produced by Booknook.biz

Also by Sam Allen

Route 66 Party Guide

Route 66 Top 10s

The Deacons of Deadwood Motorcycle Club

How to Home Distill Whiskey without Screwing It Up

Other Fun Sam Allen Route 66 Projects

Website: Route66mc.com

YouTube Channel: Route 66 Party Guide

Roku Television Channel: Route 66 Party Guide

Dedications

These stories are dedicated to all the people who started me on my motorcycle adventures and all the people who have ridden the American roads with me, most especially:

Sue Dailey, who helped me get my first motorcycle.

David Cook, who sold me my first motorcycle.

David's son Ricky Cook, who became my best friend, co-founded the Deacons of Deadwood Motorcycle Club with me and became its second President.

My brother Tolly. Riding motorcycles together changed our lives.

Carroll Kelly, who was with me on my first ride to the Sturgis Motorcycle Rally.

"Rocket" John Aubrey, John (the "Deer Slayer") Talbot and "Easy" Elza Smith, who along with Carroll Kelley and me, logged thousands of miles across the country on many trips during my early days of riding.

Mike (the "Hooligan") Callahan, with whom I've ridden across the country more times than I can remember, including a ride from Houston to Washington D.C. in under 24 hours, and a ride from Chicago to Los Angeles on old Route 66 in eight and a half days.

Peter (the "Commodore") Sommer, who rode with me to the Sturgis Rally, with a detour through Canada around the Great Lakes, and a run in with Canadian Customs officials.

Erick "ER" Robertson; Bob (the "Torch") Mitchell; Sam Douglass; Preston (the "Ghost") Douglass; and Ted Ricketson, who along with some of the guys listed above, were the original founders of the Deacons of Deadwood.

Steve ("Lambo") Lamb, who was with the Deacons from our first year and later became our President.

Past Deacons of Deadwood Presidents Jay McKendree; "Captain" Kirk Lane; Geoff ("Sandman") Seaman; David ("Hoss") Stevens and Cliff (the "Mechanic") Davis.

All the other members, past and present, of the Deacons of Deadwood Motorcycle Club, other than those who have been declared *Damnatio Memorae*.

Joe ("Cruz") Valdez and Jim ("Sprocket") Lange, who were members of the Bandidos Motorcycle Club; and the Mad Doctor, who was the National Head Photographer of *Outlaw Biker* magazine. These guys were great friends of the Deacons of Deadwood in our early years.

Kip Attaway, who I met in Jackson, Wyoming over 35 years ago before I ever fired up a motorcycle, and who became the first Honorary Member of the Deacons of Deadwood.

Brett Christensen, who helped me out when I filled my tank with diesel fuel and didn't give me the nickname "Diesel Sam."

Ken Becker, who knows everything about Route 66 and has taken me on many rides exploring now forgotten parts of it.

Steve ("Pipes") Skelton and Kim McMillen, who rode beyond the rainbow with me.

Carol Mateo, who will always be in my heart.

All of the other wonderful people who I've met over the nearly half million miles I've ridden across this beautiful land and who inspired these stories.

Contents

Dedications	vii
Foreword	xi
The Rides	**1**
Cruising in Canada with the Commodore	3
My Early Route 66 Road Trips	9
On the Road Again	16
My Kind of Town	18
Riding the Richter	21
Oatman Oasis	26
A Scary Ride	31
Cratered in Arizona	34
My Favorite Route 66 Ride	37
Rialto Reality	41
The Places and People	**45**
There Ain't no Memories in First Class	47
Dick's on 66	52
Meeting the Iron Sleds MC	54
Johnnies Bar: An Inspiration for Jerome Kern	57
Diplomatic Relations with Cuba	59
The Seaba Station Motorcycle Museum	61
John Hargrove's OK County 66 Mini Museum	64
A Visit with Blaine Davis at the Blue Whale	66
The Road Not Taken	69
Loo – Ceil, Please Come Back Where You Belong	73
Four Museums	76
What Happens in Vega Stays in Vega	78
Tucumcari Tonight	80
Climbing La Bajada Hill	83
Fire Melts the Ice in Grants	86

Wild Times in Williams	89
Victor Victoriaville	92
The Iron Hog Saloon	94
A Visit with Joe Bono	96

Route 66 History   **99**

A Brief History of Route 66	101
Happy 90th Birthday Route 66!	105
The Negro Motorist Green Book	*117*
Bonnie and Clyde on Route 66	122
The Coral Court Caper (Part 1)	128
The Coral Court Caper (Part 2)	132
Andy Warhol's Rambunctious Route 66 Ride	135
The First and Last Wild West Gunfighters	140
Sherman's Last March	144
John Chisum and the Chisholm Trail	149
Billy the Kid on Route 66	152
The Mystery of Dead Woman Crossing	159
Martin Milner RIP	162

Stories from the Heart   **165**

The Big Blink	167
Do you have any Gray Poupon?	175
Carousing with Carroll Kelly	181
Remembrances of a Friendship	186
Beyond the Rainbow	191
Respecting our Heroes at the Greatest Spectacle in Racing	196

Politically Incorrect Stories   **203**

Five Hard Men	205
10 Things You Don't Do in a Biker Bar	211
Eat Me!	214
Eat Me! Bonus	219
Drink Me!	220

Sam Allen Route 66 Projects   **225**
About the Author   **231**

Foreword

During Christmas season in 1996, I was driving my car around Houston's 610 Loop and saw a billboard for Mancuso Harley-Davidson. I thought to myself, "I can afford one of those." I called Sue Dailey, who was the only person I knew who owned a motorcycle, and she told me I needed to meet David Cook. She gave me David's phone number and told me she'd call him to give a heads-up to expect my call. I called David the next day and arranged to meet him after work.

David owned a motorcycle custom shop called Luxury Cycles Unlimited. He did custom and repair work out of his shop and also sold used motorcycles. Minutes after I arrived I had a beer in my hand and David was showing me a 1995 Harley-Davidson Road King with only 800 miles on it. He told me how good I'd look cruising through town with a hot biker babe on the back. The price was $18,000.

I told him I'd need to think about it and I'd get back to him in a day or two. He said I better get back to him quickly because a couple of other people were looking at the bike.

I left Luxury Cycles and called Sue from my car to ask her about the bike. She told me it was a great bike at a great price and that I should get it. I called David and told him I'd take the bike. He told me to bring him a certified check, which I did the next day.

I didn't know how to ride a motorcycle, so I had to go to motorcycle driving school. I wasn't able to get into a class until the middle of the following January, which was a month away. I took the class and went to Luxury Cycles to ride the bike home. He had a guy who was working for him follow me to be sure I didn't kill myself on the way. I almost dropped the bike at a stop light right before some railroad tracks, but I held it up and made it home safely.

That was the start of a change in my life. I wound up taking to riding motorcycles quickly, and later that year took my first cross country ride, which was from Houston to the Black Hills Motorcycle Rally in Sturgis, South Dakota.

When all this was going on, I was a partner in the Corporate Finance Group in one of Houston's top law firm. Practicing law kept me busy, but I made time to ride my motorcycle thousands of miles each year. I went to the west coast following Route 66 from Oklahoma City to Los Angeles. On another west coast trip I rode the entire Pacific Coast Highway.

I went to the Sturgis Rally over 10 years in a row. On those rides I went to Jackson, Wyoming; Yellowstone Park; Montana through Silvergate, over Beartooth Pass to Red Lodge, Billings, the Custer Battlefield and back into Wyoming; the Black Hills of South Dakota and through the Badlands; and to dozens of other places.

I also rode east a few times, including to New York City and through New England where I grew up.

Two thousand two was a big year. Ricky Cook and I founded the Deacons of Deadwood Motorcycle Club, which had nine founding members, with an additional four coming aboard a week later. The founders of the Deacons of Deadwood largely were the guys who had been on all those rides with me over the years after I bought that Road King from David Cook. The Club quickly grew, and we now have about 80 members. We have raised nearly $4,000,000 for charities benefiting children in the Houston area.

The next big year was 2011. In January of that year I left my law firm and went into private practice. Soon after I left the firm I drove to Chicago then spent three weeks driving on Route 66 to Los Angeles. I took notes with the thought I'd write something about the trip.

It was love at first ride. In 2012, my brother Dan and I created route66mc.com, which is a comprehensive website about Route 66.

In 2014, I published the first edition of *The Route 66 Motorcycle Party Guide*. That book now is on its third edition under the new title, *The Route 66 Party Guide*.

Foreword

In 2015, I started writing stories about my Route 66 adventures. I published them through a Go Daddy direct mail service and soon built a strong following. Many of the stories were about my rides on Route 66. Others were about the places I've been and the people I've met on those rides. I also wrote stories about Route 66 history, about famous people on Route 66 and about events that occurred on Route 66. I even wrote stories about events that happened in Route 66 towns decades before Route 66 was established.

Then there are my stories from the heart. These stories generally didn't have anything to do with Route 66 or riding motorcycles. They were about important friendships and experiences I've had. Some of these stories were so personal I almost didn't publish them. To my surprise, they turned out to be among my most well received stories.

Then there are some off color stories that might get me "canceled." We are in an era where Dr. Seuss books are getting banned or rewritten so as not to be too offensive. Under that standard, some of my stories might make the pajama clad snowflakes who foster the cancel culture from the basements of their parents houses to cower with indignation or seek the help of therapists to overcome the microaggressions that they no doubt will find in these stories.

This book collects over 50 of my favorite stories. I hope you enjoy reading them as much as I enjoyed writing them.

Sam Allen
July 4, 2023

This is my brother Tolly and me in front of Lambeau Field, where the Green Bay Packers play. Our Motorcycle Club, the Deacons of Deadwood, has a patch that Members can earn by riding their motorcycles through all of the 48 lower states. This photo was taken on a ride Tolly and I took out west to get Tolly some of the states he needed. He rode 1,250 miles from Stuart, Florida to Houston, where I live. We left from Houston and went 5,500 through Texas, then through parts of Oklahoma, Kansas, Nebraska, Colorado, New Mexico, Arizona, California, Nevada, Utah, Idaho, Wyoming, South Dakota, North Dakota, Iowa, Minnesota, Wisconsin, Michigan, Indiana, Ohio, Kentucky, Tennessee, Missouri, Arkansas and back to Texas. Tolly then rode 1,250 miles back to Florida, for total mileage of 8,000 miles. Tolly now has the patch.

Riding motorcycles together over the last couple of decades changed our lives. We are the closest of brothers and best of friends.

The Rides

Most of the stories in this chapter are about motorcycle rides I have taken on Route 66. But some of them are about how I first started exploring Route 66 before I owned a motorcycle, and about a decade long series of automobile road trips I took on Route 66 with my friend Ricky Cook.

This story is about a ride I took with my Deacons of Deadwood MC Brother Peter the "Commodore" Sommer through Canada and around the Great Lakes on our way to the Sturgis Motorcycle rally.

Cruising in Canada with the Commodore

I'VE GOT A FRIEND IN the Deacons of Deadwood Motorcycle Club we call "The Commodore" because of his commanding baritone voice and his erudite demeanor. The Commodore oversaw oil and gas acquisitions in the Western Hemisphere for Chevron before he retired to dedicate himself to more important matters, like riding motorcycles across continents.

The Commodore is one of a hand full of Deacons who has a "Hard Core" patch. I'm one too.

To earn that patch, a Member must complete three rides sanctioned by the Iron Butt Association including a Saddle Sore 1,000 (1,000 miles in 24 hours); a Bun Burner (1,500 miles in 36 hours); and at least one Extreme Ride, such as the Bun Burner Gold (1,500 miles in 24 hours). After all that, the Member needs to ride another 25,000 miles with the Deacons' other Members. The Commodore's Extreme Rides include a Border to Border (Mexico to Canada in under 36 hours) and a Coast to Coast (Atlantic to Pacific Oceans in under 48 hours).

A few years ago, The Commodore and I decided to ride through New England and Canada on our way to the Sturgis Motorcycle Rally in the Black Hills of South Dakota. I rode my bike 1,800 miles from Houston to Connecticut to see my Dear Old Mom on the way, then rode another 225 miles to Portland, Maine to meet The Commodore. Normally, The Commodore would have ridden to Maine with me, but uncharacteristically, on this trip he shipped his bike to the local Harley dealership in Portland and flew up.

When we picked up his bike, The Commodore found that he had brought the wrong keys and he could not open his saddlebags. That was a problem, because we were going to travel through several states that required helmets for motorcycle riders. He had brought two helmets, but both were in the locked saddlebags. So, he bought a third helmet to use until we met up with his keys, which he arranged to be shipped to him.

Fortunately, the ignition on his bike was not locked so he could start it.

The first day we rode in a cool and persistent rain through some beautiful green mountains in Maine and New Hampshire until we got to the Canadian border. The Canadian customs officials asked if we had any contraband in our saddlebags. I don't remember The Commodore's exact response, but so far as I can remember, he replied:

"Unfortunately, I had my motorcycle delivered to Portland, Maine, and mistakenly brought the wrong set of keys; therefore, as much as I would like to comply with your request to examine the contents of my saddlebags, I regret that will be impossible due to the obvious impediments to opening them."

"I appreciate your indefatigable efforts to secure the border of your great nation from the havoc often wrought by members of motorcycle clubs of a less genteel pedigree than ours. Nonetheless, I can assure you, on my word of honor as a former executive of the Chevron Corporation and as a Member in good standing of the Deacons of Deadwood Motorcycle Club, that my saddlebags do not contain any article or substance that would be prohibited from being transported into Canada, or that would pose any danger to its citizens, its wildlife or its environmental purity."

"So, kind Sirs, we will be on our way. Tally Ho!"

The customs official replied: "You guys pull in over there."

The Canadian customs officials examining The Commodore's bike were pretty good guys. Rather than drilling out Peter's locks, they took some care in unbolting the hardware so they could examine the contents of the saddlebags without damaging anything. The process took several hours, and when we were done, The Commodore and I presumed we could be on our way. We were wrong.

Earlier in the process, a female customs official asked for my Cut (biker lingo for a motorcycle club member's vest and patch). It turned out that while The Commodore's bike was being disassembled, the customs babe was doing a background check on the Deacons of Deadwood MC and me.

I was escorted into a room that looked like something from *Law and Order*. The room was stark. The lone chair and table in the room were bolted to the floor. There was a loop where a person being interrogated could be handcuffed to the table, but they did not cuff me. The customs babe said that before The Commodore and I could leave, I would have to explain the meaning of each of the Deacons patches on my Cut.

I told her that wouldn't be a problem because I had designed all of them.

The process went well until she asked about a round patch about two inches in diameter with a white background and black number 19 in the center. The 19 Patch is our most secret award. It is so secret that those in the Club who have not earned it do not know what it means. If a Member satisfies the requirements, those of us who have the patch bestow it on the Member who earned it.

I explained all of this to the custom's babe, and told her that because of its confidential nature, I would rather not explain its meaning. She was insistent. She asked whether it stood for having to kill 19 people before being patched in as a Deacon.

I told her that the Deacons were lovers not fighters and that she should check out our website to verify that. She told me she had checked, but she couldn't be sure that the web site wasn't a front for a criminal enterprise. In the end, I had to explain the meaning of the patch, but it's still a secret so I can't tell you what it means. Suffice it to say that no killings or drugs are involved, and the illegality, if any, would relate to a victimless crime.

After The Commodore and I finally cleared the border, we rode through a large traffic jam in Montréal. It was still raining and getting dark. We stopped at a gas station and asked if there was a national chain hotel nearby. The gas station attendant said it was a long way away. That worried us. We thought we might have to go to Ottawa or some other distant location off our planned route. It turned out there was a Holiday Inn about ten miles away.

We made it to the hotel as nighttime settled in. When we got there, we found that the hotel had a conclave of catholic Nuns staying there, and there also was a bagpipe convention going on. You really can't make this stuff up.

After an evening of beer at the bar and bagpipe serenades through the night, we rode around Lake Superior with an overnight stay in Thunder Bay. From there we rode back into the United States in Minnesota. US Customs welcomed us home without the scrutiny we had experienced while entering Canada. We rode across Minnesota to Bismarck, North Dakota, which was so small we couldn't see it from the highway. The next day we cruised into Deadwood.

On our first night in Deadwood, I was in a spot called Miss Molly's. Molly's is across the street from the Bullock Hotel, which had been owned and operated by Seth Bullock, Deadwood's first sheriff.

A former Deacon came in, but it wasn't a pleasant thing. We had booted him out the previous year for being an asshole and declared him to be *Damnatio Memorae*. Since he was *damnatio memorae*, I refused to greet him by name. Instead, I told him that I had gone to a lot of trouble not to have to associate with him in Texas, and that I sure wasn't going to associate with him in South Dakota. It was awkward, but it worked out OK.

After two nights in Deadwood, The Commodore, a couple of other Deacons and I rode 375 miles in the rain to Denver, where we treated ourselves to a night and dinner at the Brown Palace Hotel. From there, The Commodore and I spent two days riding a bit over 1,000 miles back to Houston.

We did not do any Iron Butts, but it was an honest ride of over 4,500 miles in 10 days, not counting my additional 2,100 miles from Houston to Portland.

The Commodore is planning a ride to the Arctic Circle this summer. I'll be passing on that one.

Endnote: *The Commodore and Ben "Wildman" Thompson made that ride to the Arctic Circle. It turned out that the roads up there were not safe for motorcycles. They rode "Slingshots," which are open cockpit, two seat vehicles with two wheels in the front and one in the back. I'd sure like to make that trip one of these days.*

Ricky Cook and I have traveled thousands of miles together over the last three decades. We founded the Deacons of Deadwood Motorcycle Club in 2002 with nine Members. We now have over 80 members and we have donated nearly $4,000,000 to charities benefiting children in the Houston area. This is Ricky and me at a Deacons of Deadwood meeting on April 1, 2023.

The Rides

My Early Route 66 Road Trips

During most of the 1980s I practiced law in New York City. It was an exciting time called the Decade of Greed because of all the hostile corporate takeovers that took place. Financier Ivan Boesky proclaimed that "Greed is good", then went to prison for securities fraud. I was working in the World Trade Center at a old-line law firm. I traveled the country working on sophisticated deals with smart people, many of whom remain friends over four decades later. I had New York Yankees season tickets. Life was glorious. Then for reasons that seemed clear at the time, I moved to Houston, Texas on January 2, 1990.

One of the first things I did was buy a fire engine red Ford Mustang convertible with a V-8 engine and a six-speed manual transmission. When I wasn't working, I would drive around the country, and I found I had an explorer's heart. I liked to take random trips with only the outline of a destination, and sometimes those travels would take me to Route 66. I vaguely understood I was on a special road, but Route 66 never was a destination in itself.

About 20 years ago, I was a bit burned out at work and decided to drive west during Thanksgiving week. It was the first time I had gone out of my way to travel on Route 66. I drove to Oklahoma City, which was the nearest Route 66 town, and headed toward Gallup, New Mexico. I picked Gallup because I had wondered through there a few years previously and found the El Rancho Hotel, which had a unique lobby and a bar that *Esquire Magazine* ranked in the Top 50 Bars in the United States. Every room was named after a movie star who had stayed there. Unfortunately, on that first visit the El Rancho was sold out so I wound up at a Holiday Inn. The Thanksgiving trip offered me another chance to stay there.

I wound up making a Thanksgiving trip to Gallup an annual event. I became friends with El Rancho owner Armond Ortega and Dahlia the bartender, who weighed about 100 pounds despite having 10 children. The El Rancho staff came to know me and would set aside the Kirk Douglas Room for me each Thanksgiving weekend. Plus, even though the bar was closed on Thanksgiving Day, they would open it for me so I could watch the Ole Miss-Mississippi State football game on their big screen TV.

Those trips were peaceful, and I looked upon them as personal retreats that allowed me to recharge before facing the Christmas Season and end of year rush of work.

Then David Cook died in October 14, 2001.

David was a professional con man who conned his friends every day. But if a friend was in need, he was there to help, although the assistance of one friend likely would be affected by conning another, and David for sure would make money on the deal. He sold me my first motorcycle and conned me on repairs and unneeded service for years after that, but like everybody else, I loved him.

I'd met David's son Rickey a year or so after I met David, and Ricky had become my best friend in Houston. When David died, I thought hard about whether to ask Ricky to join me on my annual Thanksgiving trip. I didn't want to turn my retreat into a cross country boozy binge. But I risked it and asked Ricky to go.

Ricky is a bright guy, but so far as I can tell, he's never read a book. He learns everything he knows by watching TV. On the other hand, I read every day and watch little TV except the news and old movies. So, it worked out great when we decided to pass the driving time by listening to audio books. We would ride for hours without talking except while changing the discs to the books.

But we hit a few high notes at night. We made it to the El Rancho the third day out. We had dinner there and poured down a few at the bar. I introduced Ricky to Mr. Ortega and Dahlia, and we had our picture taken with them.

After the El Rancho Bar, we walked down the street to Goodfella's Bar. If you ever want to pick up a Navajo chick, Goodfella's is the place to be. It was packed, and other than one blond babe, Ricky and I were the only two gringos. And the blond chick was dipping Skoll.

They had karaoke going on, so I signed up to sing Petula Clark's song *Downtown*. I know that sounds an odd song for a guy to sing, but I had alternate lyrics that my friend, singer songwriter Kip Attaway, uses in his show:

🎵🎵🎵 *The queers and the pimps are there;*
You know when you see folks with spiked purple hair; that you're
Down-Town, out where the perverts are;
Down-Town, somebody stole my car;
Down-Town, somebody's following you 🎵🎵🎵

Suffice it to say, the rest of Kip's lyrics are even racier than these.

I made it through most of the first verse before the crowd started noticing my lyrics. People began to stir. Some of them laughed, but others were aghast. Someone from the back of the room yelled: "Turn it off! He's going to do it again!"

They unplugged me. Ricky and I were banned from singing, but being among the few people spending money, we weren't booted out.

We closed Goodfella's down. I thought Ricky had a chance with the blond chick, but he struck out and we headed in.

When we got back to the El Rancho, there was no one in the lobby except the guy at the check in desk, and he was snoozing. There was a coin operated player piano in the lobby, and either Ricky or I put a quarter in the slot. We expected a snappy tune, but this thing started playing so abruptly and loudly that the guy behind the desk jumped straight up about three feet like a scared cat. We couldn't get the piano to stop playing, and we woke up half the hotel. Within a few seconds there were hotel guests looking at us from the balcony overlooking the lobby. We made hasty exits to our rooms.

The next morning there was tape over the coin slot on the piano.

From Gallup we headed to Tombstone, Arizona, where we planned to spend a couple of days. Tombstone is the site of the Shoot-Out at the OK Corral and the home of the Wild West's first Boot Hill Cemetery,

Ricky Cook and me in the Lobby of the El Rancho Hotel in Gallup, New Mexico. Ricky and I went there for Thanksgiving Day for over a decade. The other people in the photo are Armond Ortega, who owned the El Rancho; Dalia the bartender, who would open up the El Rancho Bar just for us on Thanksgiving Day so we could watch the Ole Miss – Mississippi State football game, and Dalia's son. This photo has been on my wall for nearly 20 years.

and we were looking forward to visiting both. Plus, there is not an edible bite of food in Gallup, so we figured we'd have a nice Thanksgiving meal in Tombstone.

Most of Tombstone burned down in 1882, but there are a few original buildings. The site of the Shoot-Out at the OK Corral isn't one of them.

The shoot-out occurred on October 26, 1881. Wyatt Earp, his brothers Virgil and Morgan, and Doc Holiday walked from the Oriental Saloon down Allen Street, then rounded the corner and went up Freemont Street, which is parallel to Allen Street. They confronted Ike and Billy Clanton, Tom and Frank McLaury and Billy Claiborne, all of whom had been bragging that they were going to shoot it out with the Earps.

The gunfight took place in a narrow lot next to C.S. Fly's Photographic Studio, which was six doors down from the back entrance to the O.K. Corral. It lasted fewer than 30 seconds. Tom and Frank McLaury and Billy Clanton were killed. Virgil and Morgan Earp were wounded.

The Bird Cage Theater survived the fire. It was a saloon, gambling hall and brothel that opened on December 26, 1881. Wyatt Earp's common law wife Josie worked there. There was live entertainment on a stage on the main floor. Box seats, or "Bird Cages" overlooked the floor, and curtains could be drawn for privacy.

They had a poker game that went on 24 hours a day, for eight years, five months and three days. The buy in was $10,000, which would be approximately $227,000 in 2018 dollars. The game stopped only because the business shut down in 1892. Once closed, the building was not reopened until 1934, and the new owners were delighted to find that nothing had been touched since the closing. The cards and chips being used for the last hand of the poker game still were on the table. Over 120 bullet holes were found throughout the building. It's now a museum and they don't serve alcohol.

Big Nose Kate's Saloon is down the street from the Bird Cage, and they do serve alcohol. It is named for Mary Katherine ("Big Nose Kate") Horony-Cummings, who was a Tombstone prostitute and Doc Holiday's common law wife. The saloon is in the lobby of the Grand Hotel, which once was the finest hotel between San Francisco and Tombstone. The Hotel burned down in the 1882 fire. The original bar survived and now is in use on the rebuilt first floor. Wyatt Earp and his brothers and Doc Holiday all drank off that wood.

Everybody in Tombstone dresses like it's the 1880s. The men carry loaded Colt 45 Peacemakers on gun belts, and the guns must be checked when going into a bar.

Ricky and I were unarmed, but when we walked into Big Nose Kate's, we both were wearing cowboy hats and boots. I had a duster and red paisley vest. I sidled up to the bar, and when the bartender came over, I tossed out a silver dollar I had brought for the occasion and said "Whiskey. Leave the bottle." The guy looked at me like I was the asshole of the year, and I said "Hey man. I just always wanted to do that."

We drank at Big Nose Kate's for a while then went to a bar across the street that is on the site of the Campbell & Hatch Billiard Parlor, where Morgan Earp was assassinated on March 18, 1882, less than six months after the Shoot-Out at the O.K. Corral. We met a bunch of kids from Germany who were traveling from Los Angeles to New York. They all had straw cowboy hats that looked like they had been stolen from migrant workers. Ricky and I bought them a bunch of shots of whiskey, and Rickey gave all of them some Skoll, which made a few of them puke Maybe it was the whiskey; who knows. There was a stuffed buffalo in there, and one of the German's hopped on top of it like it was bucking bull. He waived his hat and yelled "Look, Sammy. I am cowboy!"

Boot Hill is on the outskirts of town. It was established in 1878, and after 1883, it was used exclusively for outlaws. There are about 250 graves made by stacking stones over the corpses. The markers all are replicas. The graves of Tom and Frank McLaury and Billy Clanton are there. So is the marker featured in the movie *Tombstone*:

> "Here lies Lester Moore.
> Four slugs from a 44.
> No Les, no More."

My favorite:

> "Here lies George Johnson,
> hanged by mistake 1882.
> He was right, we were wrong.
> But we strung him up and now he's gone."

On our first night in Tombstone, we discovered that the food was only marginally better than the food in Gallup. We decided to have Thanksgiving dinner in Bisbee, which in on the Mexican border about 20 miles south of Tombstone. Bisbee is an Old West mining town with a huge open pit copper mine in downtown. It also is kind of a hippy place with many artists. It must be the gayest town per capita in Arizona.

Ricky and I checked into the Copper Queen Hotel, which had the best restaurant in Bisbee. We didn't have reservations so we had to wait at the bar for a while. When we were seated, Ricky went to the men's room. The waiter asked me if I wanted to order a cocktail or whether I wanted to wait for my "companion" to return. I let that pass and ordered us a couple of beers.

We had an excellent meal at the Copper Queen and headed back toward Houston the next day. We made it to El Paso without getting on a major highway. On the way we passed a huge monument in the middle of nowhere, which turned out to be the site where Geronimo surrendered to General Nelson Miles on September 6, 1886.

We went to a bar in Downtown El Paso that I've been hitting for years, but I can never remember its name. It's a block or so down the street from the site of the Acme Saloon, where Old West gunslinger John Wesley Hardin was killed by lawman John Selman on August 19, 1895. The coroner said the "Other than being dead he is in excellent condition."

At his trial, Selman claimed self-defense; *however*, some of the witnesses claimed Selman shot Hardin in the back. The judge said "If he shot him from the front it was good shooting. If he shot him from behind it was good judgment!"

The next morning, we drove 750 miles from El Paso to Houston, listening to audio books the whole way.

Rickey and I went west during Thanksgiving week for over a decade. Although we didn't go to the same places every time, we always took Route 66 to Gallup. The guy we scared with the player piano still snoozes through the night shift at the El Rancho Hotel, and the piano still has tape over the coin slot. Dahlia now works at the Fire Rock Navajo Casino, just East of Gallup, and we run into her on occasion. Mr. Ortega has died. The photo of the four of us still hangs in my apartment.

This story came about when I was getting ready to leave on a ride on which I was going to produce a pilot TV show about riding motorcycles on Route 66. Several other stories in this collection were written during that trip.

On the Road Again

On the road again
Goin' places that I've never been
Seeing places I may never see again
Oh I can't wait to get on the road again.

—Willie Nelson

There is nothing quite like the feeling I get when I'm leaving town on a 6,000 mile motorcycle ride knowing that I won't be back for weeks. I usually have an itinerary, but it's more of a guideline than a schedule.

One of the freedoms of a long ride is that it can be changed on a whim. I once was on my way to the Black Hills Motorcycle Rally in Sturgis South Dakota. I had a date on the back of my bike, and we both had been to Sturgis before. When we got to Dallas, rather than heading north on I-35 toward York, Nebraska, which was our destination that day, I headed east on I-20. My date tapped me on the shoulder and asked where we were going. I told her we were headed to New York City. Riding a motorcycle into the City through the Lincoln Tunnel is a kick.

I had been riding over chunks of Route 66 for years, but I never had traveled its entire length on a single trip. In January 2011, I got the chance. I thought Route 66 would be clearly marked the whole way and easy to find. Well, I was wrong about the ease with which I could find Route 66. I made it from Chicago to Santa Monica, but there were sections of the route I couldn't find so there were gaps I never saw. That made me want to go back to find the places I had missed.

Over time, I learned that Route 66 had been realigned many times, and that other than when it opened in 1926, there has never been a single Route 66.

I've spent the last several years exploring the places I've never been. I've found many famous attractions that are as glorious as advertised. But while many Route 66 attractions have retained their original aura, more of them disappear each year. Many traditional Route 66 sites are just plain tired. There are motels and restaurants that have become "classics" because they survived rather than surviving because they were classics.

But there is still much to see. There are lonely strips of concrete that stripe long forgotten byways. There are small and large towns still displaying the colorful neon signs of the old motels and restaurants where the prosperous would stay during their adventures west, or where families would stay on their way to search for better lives.

You can feel the history. You can feel what it must have been like to travel Route 66 when it was the gateway to the west. Although physical things are disappearing, the history and the people are still there for those with enough of an adventurous spirit to find them.

I have one of those adventurous spirits.

The day after tomorrow I'm leaving on my bike to ride Route 66 again to film a Pilot TV show about riding motorcycles on Route 66. I wish I was leaving this minute. The trip is scheduled for 27 days. I have a day to day itinerary. I'll follow it for the first week because I'll have a film crew and cast members traveling with me during that time. But once the primary filming has been completed, I'll have nearly three weeks to make it to Santa Monica and back to Houston. I suspect the itinerary will become a guideline and I'll concentrate on finding new places to see and new people to meet.

Thank goodness there is no one Route 66. It gives me a lifetime of places to explore.

This story is about the beginning of my ride to produce a Pilot TV show called "Kicks on 66," which is about riding motorcycles on Route 66. I headed to Chicago with my Deacons of Deadwood MC brother, Justin the "Kid" Dossett, and a videographer named Greg Sitler. We met my MC Brothers "Captain" Kirk Lane and Rodney "Rodney King" Fields, in Wilmington, Illinois, home of the Gemini Giant. They had ridden from Deadwood, South Dakota in one day to join our film crew.

The idea was to film our activities every day as we rode down Route 66 until the money ran out. We made it as far as St Robert, Missouri. Everybody else headed home, but I continued on Route 66 all the way to Los Angeles.

My Kind of Town

You have to love a motorcycle ride where you need to go almost 1,200 miles just to get to the start.

I headed to Chicago a couple of days ago with Justin "the Kid" Dossett and Greg Sitler, who is the videographer for my project to produce a Pilot TV show about riding motorcycles on Route 66. The Kid and I were on bikes and Greg followed in my Jeep. It was one of those rides we just needed to grind out. Set the cruise control on 80 miles per hour and put pavement behind us.

We rode 600 miles to Memphis the first day. The ride through Texas was pretty good. There were a bunch of small towns along the way that broke up the trip, and there was some nice terrain that was fun on a motorcycle. But once we got past Texarkana, it was harsh. I don't understand heat indexes that calculate what the temperature "feels like." The temperature just is what it is. The thermometer on my bike showed a road temperature of 110 degrees, and it felt like 110 degrees.

When we were exiting I-30 onto I-40 just outside of Little Rock, I hit a bump hard. I almost was thrown from my bike, and I jammed my back. It was painful, and the pain has worsened. Folks in the entertainment industry will tell performers to "break a leg," but "break a back" would be a bit much.

Anyway, we made it to Memphis. I figured that cold beer would be the best remedy to ease the pain in my back, so we hit the hotel bar for a few frosties, and then walked next door to the Rendezvous for some ribs and more beer. The Rendezvous probably is the most famous Bar-B-Q place in Memphis, and Memphis is the Bar-B-Q capital of the galaxy. I've had better Bar-B-Q, but I don't know that I've ever had more fun eating it than at the Rendezvous.

After dinner, my back was still killing me, so a more potent anesthetic was needed. We headed to Beale Street for some blues and whiskey. As it turned out, we were so exhausted from riding in the heat we had one pop and headed to the hotel for some sleep.

The next day we rode 550 miles to Chicago. It was warm, but we were spared the heat of the previous day. It was 90 degrees and it felt like 90 degrees.

As we were pulling into town on Lake Shore Drive, the Kid's bike broke down and we blocked traffic for a while. Fortunately, he got the bike started and made it to the hotel, but he spent the whole next day trying to get it repaired. He made two trips to the Harley shop, and the bike still was not running right. But at least it was running.

We started filming our TV Pilot that same day. It mostly was taking some stock footage on Route 66 in Chicago and Cicero. In Cicero, we interviewed the owner of Henry's, where the colorful sign says, "It's a Meal in Itself." Henry's has been serving hot dogs on Route 66 for over 65 years. The current owners bought it from the original Henry's son almost 30 years ago.

The owner told us she really didn't know much about Route 66 and how it had changed over the years. Then in the course of the interview, she told us a bunch of history about Henry's and the neighborhood it's in. For instance, there is a classic roadside attraction in Atlanta, Illinois, called the Bunyon Giant. It's a 22 foot tall statue of a guy holding a giant hot dog. I knew that it before it was moved to Atlanta, it was at Bunyon's drive-in restaurant in Cicero; *however*, I've never known where

Bunyon's was. As it turns out, it was just down the street from Henry's, and the building is still there housing a Mexican restaurant.

The next day we head out on Route 66 in earnest. Once we got outside of the Chicago metropolitan area, we rode through the beginning of the small towns for which Route 66 is famous. We would be meeting my MC brothers "Captain Kirk" Lane and Rodney "King" Fields that night who joined our film crew. We won't be on another interstate highway until just outside Tucumcari, New Mexico.

The real adventure is about to begin!

Endnote: I did produce the "Kicks on 66" Pilot. I sent it to several independent production companies to see if they would finance a more polished video and try to sell it to a television network. The Pilot received significant consideration but we were unable to get a network to pick it up. But you can see it on my YouTube Channel, "Route 66 Party Guide'" if you follow this link: bit.ly/3ZvBwRK.

The Pilot finally made it onto a television network. You can see it on my Roku Channel, "Route 66 Party Guide", along with nearly 100 other videos I produced about riding motorcycles on Route 66.

This blog has some stories about my friend Heidi. One of them happened in St. Louis, but other than this slim connection with Route 66, these are not Route 66 stories; however, they are fun.

Riding the Richter

I DON'T REMEMBER HOW or when I met my friend Heidi, but it was before I founded the Deacons of Deadwood Motorcycle Club in 2002. We've never actually dated, but we've always been wonderful friends. Heidi is getting married next week to Roy Smith. Her upcoming nuptials made me recall some of the motorcycle trips we took together, and Heidi has given me permission to tell a couple of them here. So, this blog goes out as a big Congrats to Heidi and Roy.

Roy, you are getting a hell of a gal!

* * *

Heidi always was up for a long ride on short notice. Over a decade ago, some friends and I were out at some bar. We decided to make a last-minute trip to the Sturgis Motorcycle Rally. We had no hotel reservations, so we were going to head to the Black Hills and hope for the best.

I called Heidi in the middle of the night and asked if she wanted to go. She asked when we would be leaving. I told her at 4:00 that morning. She asked when we would be back. I said I wasn't sure. She said she was in.

The group included Carroll Kelly and his girlfriend Ann.

"Rocket John" Aubrey came along. He's the Rocket because if he can get his motorcycle to start, he rides as fast as a rocket. I don't remember if his wife Amy came, but she loves long rides and if she wasn't with us in person she was in spirit.

"Disco John" Talbot was with us. He's Disco John because of his fancy dance moves. We also call him the "Deer Slayer" because once on

This is my friend Heidi and me at a Deacons of Deadwood Charity Ball. For obvious reasons, when she walks it can be measured on the Richter Scale. We've ridden thousands of miles together.

a ride to Big Bend State Park in South Texas he hit a deer at 85 miles an hour and lived to tell about it.

Heidi and I rounded out the crew.

We left Houston as scheduled with the goal of reaching York, Nebraska, which was about halfway between Houston and Deadwood. But when we got to York, Nebraska, we decided to push on to North Platte, South Dakota, which was Buffalo Bill's hometown. We got there at about 10:00 at night, and without intending to do it, we found we had completed an Iron Butt Bun Burner ride, which is 1,000 miles in under 24 hours.

Number of miles: 1,050.
Hours of riding:15
Bitching by Heidi: Zero.

We cruised into Deadwood the next afternoon, rode around the Black Hills a bit, stayed one more day then rode two days back to Houston.

* * *

A few years later, I decided to try to map Route 66 through St. Louis. I had not yet written *The Route 66 Party Guide*, but my website, *Route66mc.com* was up and running, and I knew my directions through St. Louis needed help.

By this time Heidi had moved from Houston to Nashville. I called her to see if she wanted to drive up to St. Louis to meet me for a few days of riding through the Ozarks. She said she was in.

There is a Holiday Inn in St. Louis on Route 66 near where the iconic Coral Court Motel once stood. The Holiday Inn had a fun biker themed bar called Club 277, because it was off I-44 Exit 277, and that's where Heidi was to meet me.

I got in at about 7:00. Heidi was scheduled to arrive by 10:00. So, I worked out a bit in the hotel gym and headed to Club 277 for some dinner and a couple of cold ones. I started off with a few Miller Lites. I ordered some chicken noodle soup and pot roast and washed it down with some pinot grigio. After dinner, I ratcheted up to double Turkey and sodas and settled in to listen to the band and wait for Heidi.

She got in a little over an hour late, but by the time she arrived, I was only on my third Turkey, so I was reasonably sober and in an excellent mood. Heidi ordered a mojito, and while she was on her second one, an unordered double Turkey showed up. Some guy at the bar I didn't know had bought it for me and he came over to chat.

I don't know why he bought one for me and not for Heidi. She's 4'11" tall and has a set of natural 44G's (that's not a typo). When she giggles them across the country on the back of a motorcycle the rumble can be measured on the Richter Scale. By the way, she also has an MBA and works for one of the biggest real estate companies in the United States.

The guy had weird hair. Less than Richard Nixon but more than Don Rickles.

Well, I drank the Turkey and I reciprocated by buying him a drink. Courvoisier, if you can believe that! I should have known I was in trouble.

Closing time crept up, so I ordered one more and asked for my tab. The guy insisted on picking up my entire bill, and over my protestations, the bartender let him do it.

Then the shooters started arriving. We started with a Jaeger. Then the bartender bought us all a starburst. Then there was some Rumplemintz, followed by a strait Turkey shooter. After that, we had a Grand Marnier shooter. I don't remember if there were any more shooters, but the bartender gave me a double Turkey and soda to go, and Heidi and I went to the room.

I woke up in the middle of the night with dry mouth and decided I needed a Coke, so I walked to the vending machine by the elevators. Unfortunately, I forgot to put my clothes on, so I was naked and I didn't have any money with me. I also didn't have my room key. That was a bigger problem than you might expect because I forgot my room number. I went to the room I thought I was in and knocked on the door. It turned out to be the wrong room. Fortunately, the guy who answered the door didn't seem too impressed. Anyway, he must not have been gay because he didn't invite me in.

The implications of my situation started to set in. I was going to have to keep knocking on doors in the hope that I would find the right room, and then hope Heidi would hear me and open the door. The prospect of knocking on more wrong doors and getting arrested as a pervert or being invited in for a reaming was not too appealing. The other alternative was calling the front desk, which also was not very appealing.

Fortunately, the next door I tried was the right one and Heidi let me in. I got in bed and fell asleep immediately. The next morning, I had forgotten the whole episode until I saw my half-finished Turkey and soda on the nightstand.

There is a moral to this story. Always keep some emergency Coca Cola in your hotel room.

This story tells about my first ride over the Oatman Highway on Route 66, but I took a circuitous route. I started in Houston, Texas, and rode to see the Indianapolis 500. From there, I rode to Ely, Nevada; through Death Valley and across Cajon Pass on the way to Laguna Niguel, California. After that I headed, back east from the California coast across the Mojave Desert to the Oatman Highway and Kingman, Arizona; and then back to Houston.

You'll hear more about the Oatman Highway in the stories that follow this one.

Oatman Oasis

After last week's post about my visit to Victorville, California, I received a nice note from Bob Kikkert, who is from Ontario. I interviewed Bob by the pool at the Wigwam Motel in Rialto, California a couple of years ago when I was filming *Kicks on Route 66*, which is about riding motorcycles on Route 66. The year before I met Bob, he and his son traveled to Chicago and rode their motorcycles to Santa Monica on Route 66. When I met Bob, he and his wife were back on Route 66 visiting Kumar Patel, the erudite proprietor of the Wigwam.

The day before our interview, Bob and his wife had ridden their motorcycle to Oatman, Arizona. He commented that the Oatman Highway is difficult riding and that "You need to know what you're doing up there." His remark was spot on, and it reminded me of my first ride to Oatman. It was a stop on of one of the best rides I've ever taken.

The ride started on May 29, 1999, three years before I founded the Deacons of Deadwood Motorcycle Club and over a dozen years before I started exploring Route 66 in a serious way. The ultimate destination was my law firm's annual Partners Retreat, which was being held at a resort in Laguna Nigel, California. But I had a few stops planned along the way.

Five of us left Houston and headed to the Indianapolis 500. We rode 600 miles the first day to Memphis, where we gobbled up ribs at the world-famous Rendezvous, then guzzled beer on Beale Street, which is the Memphis version of Bourbon Street.

The next day we rode another 500 miles to Lebanon, Ohio. Some of us stayed with my brother Ted, while others stayed at the Golden Lamb Hotel, which opened in 1803 and has hosted nine US Presidents, along with Charles Dickens, Mark Twain, Harriet Beecher Stowe and other luminaries. I don't have any stroke there and always seem to get the Martin van Buren Room.

Ted hosted a cookout for us, where I nearly burned his house down while I was trying to cook burgers.

The next day we headed to the Speedway, which is only 70 miles from my brother's house. The deal at "The Race" is that fans can bring their own beer in. There are coolers we have been using for years that fit nicely under our seats. Plus, we buy a couple of extra seats to hold our coolers so we can have better leg room. That really pisses off other folks in the stands who are looking for whatever wiggle room they can find. The coolers hold exactly 22 cans of beer, and everybody brings their own cooler. We each drink at least two on the way to the Speedway, drink a few more while tailgating and drink the rest during the Race. There never is any left over.

When the race finished, everyone else headed back to Texas, but I headed toward my Partners Retreat in California. I rode across the northern plains and wound up in Ely Nevada, where I stayed at the Nevada Hotel and Gambling Hall. The rooms are named for famous people who stayed there. I was in the Tennessee Ernie Ford Room. Ely is a small but apparently rough town. They night I got there some guy who was jealous of his girlfriend's flirting ways walked into a bar and pumped a few shotgun blasts into her.

The next morning, I planned to ride the remaining 550 miles to Laguna Niguel, California. Even though it was the beginning of June it was 27° the morning I left Ely. Ely is in the middle of nowhere, so before I left I checked a map to see where the nearest gas likely would be. It was nearly 200 miles away, and my bike had a range of about 160 miles, so I bought a couple of plastic one-gallon gas jugs, strapped them to my bike and took off.

I headed south and decided to take a detour through Death Valley. I rode to the rim, and from there the whole Valley was visible. On top of the Valley the sky was blue, and the air was crisp and clear. But the bottom of the Valley was covered by a heavy haze. I could see the one road going from my perch through the center of Death Valley until it disappeared out the other end. Down I went.

Death Valley has the lowest elevation in the United States and is its hottest place. The temperature got hot quickly as I descended. There is a resort with a golf course down there and I stopped to get some cold water. The thermometer outside the restaurant read 122°. I never felt endangered, but I recognized that if I broke down or got stranded I wouldn't survive long without water. Fortunately, I had packed plenty on my bike.

After getting out of Death Valley, I headed toward Los Angeles. When I was going over Cajon Pass the temperature was around 45° and it was raining. I arrived at Laguna Niguel in the early evening and the temperature was in the mid-70s. So that day I went from 27° in Ely, to 122° in Death Valley, to 45° over Cajon Pass, to 75° in Laguna Niguel.

The hotel was nice. Everything was for sale. If you used the soap in the shower, you paid for it. You could buy the bathrobe in your room, which I did. You could buy the bed and sheets you were sleeping on, which I didn't.

The next day I went to the pool for lunch after playing golf in the morning. All my partners knew I had a bunch of tattoos, but they all were above a golf shirt sleeve level, so they never had seen them. I could feel everybody looking at me in the hope I'd get into the pool and show the tattoos. I decided to keep the mystery.

After a few days of sun, sand, and golf in Southern California, hopped on my bike to head back to Houston. I had flown in a friend of the female persuasion as my guest at the Retreat, and she was going to ride back to Houston with me. We left Laguna Niguel in glorious weather, but soon we were in the Mojave Desert, which seemed as hot as Death Valley, only the ride across California was a lot longer.

We stopped in Newberry Springs California for some water and rest. It was so hot that I bought a bag of ice and stuffed it inside my motorcycle vest and all my pockets. We also bought a bag of ice and put it between us. All of that melted in under an hour.

We stopped again for water Needles, California, which bills itself as the second hottest place in the United States after Death Valley. We were icing up again when someone at the gas station suggested we go to Oatman, Arizona, which was close by and at an elevation high enough that it would be cool. That's where we headed.

To get there we had to take the Oatman Highway. It connects Topok, Arizona on the California border to Kingman, Arizona, over Siltgreaves Pass along the original 1926 alignment of Route 66. It turned out to be the most challenging road I've ever traversed. The lanes are narrow and there are no guard rails. If the speed limit is 10 mph, you better go five. If you go over the edge, that's it for you.

On the other hand, the vistas are beautiful, and as advertised, it was cool up there.

Oatman is an old mining town named for Olive Oatman. Olive was born in Illinois in 1837. Her family was killed near Oatman in 1851, when she was 14. She was captured by a Native American tribe, which enslaved her and sold her to the Mojave People, who tattooed her in the Mojave tradition. She eventually was set free, and she died in Sherman, Texas in 1903.

We stopped at the bar in the Oatman Hotel, which opened in 1902 as the Drulin Hotel. Clark Gable and Carole Lombard stayed there when they were married in Kingman, Arizona in 1939. The room where they stayed is on display, but the Hotel no longer serves guests.

We went straight to the bar, which was the only air-conditioned room within 50 miles. The final round of golf's U.S. Open was on the TV, and we stayed to watch Payne Stewart sink a 15-foot putt for birdie on the 18th hole to win by one stroke. As it happened, Stewart was killed in a freak airplane accident a few months later while he was on the way to play in the Tour Championship at Champions Golf Club in Houston, where I was a member.

There are no operating hotels in Oatman, so once the golf tournament was over and the sun was setting, we headed down the other side of the Oatman Highway to Kingman, where we stayed for the night.

I don't remember anything else about that ride but hearing from Bob Kikkert reminded me of the Oatman Highway and the oasis it offered on that hot Sunday afternoon.

The weather is a big part of riding a motorcycle across the country. You don't ride through the environment – you ride in it. This story is one version of the kind of thing that all hard core bikers face now and then. It's all part of the adventure.

A Scary Ride

Last week I rode from Albuquerque to Winslow, Arizona. It was only about 250 miles, but it took a whole day.

I had been sticking exclusively to old Route 66, which means I had to pass through, rather than go around, many small towns. I tried to get through Albuquerque at the beginning of rush hour. I didn't think it would be tough, but it was over two hours of stop and go traffic. I was only about a mile from getting through town when my oil light started blinking. I decided to look for a saloon and have a beer while my bike's engine cooled off. Unfortunately, I had not found a saloon when I lost all compression on my clutch.

I let the bike sit for an hour and the compression returned. I thought about heading to Grants, New Mexico, which was only 60 miles away. But for once in my life I did the prudent rather than the impulsive thing. I turned my bike around and checked into a hotel in downtown Albuquerque, which was only a few miles away.

The next morning my clutch seemed fine, so I took Central Avenue out of town. Central was part of Route 66 from 1936 until the Route was decommissioned in 1985. It passes through the heart of downtown Albuquerque then continues through "Old Town" before intersecting with I-40 at the Route 66 Casino in Rio Puerco. Once there, I had to get on I-40.

I got back on the Old Road in Mesita and started along one of my favorite stretches of Route 66. It is a winding road through sublime red rock mesas, and it passes through many Pueblos and Native American communities.

I had ridden through Mesita, Laguna, New Laguna, Paraje and Budville when a light rain came up. Rain can be refreshing when riding across deserts because it rarely lasts long, and it keeps you cool. This rain started coming down pretty hard, so I stopped at the Trading Post in Cubero, New Mexico, and did what most hard-core bikers would do. I bought a bottle of water, pulled out my iPad, uploaded David Balducci's new novel and started reading while waiting for the rain to pass.

While I was at the Trading Post, three couples from Spain rode in. They had rented Harleys in Chicago and were riding to Santa Monica. I gave them some Route 66 MC patches, and they immediately recognized them because they were using my web site, *route66mc.com*, as their guide. They all (including the women) thought that the scantily clad chick on my logo was hot-hot-hot!

The rain started to let up so I left my Barthalona Bruthas behind and headed west. I was in and out of light rain and enjoyed the cool weather through Grants, Milan, Prewitt, Thoreau, Continental Divide, Gallup, Defiance and Manuelito to the Arizona border. That's where things got exciting.

I was about 25 miles into Arizona on I-40 again because there was a gap in the Old Road. I still was riding in and out of light rain when without warning it started to fall so hard I could not see.

I have been through this before. Riding blind at 80 miles an hour on an interstate highway is precarious. You know you have to slow down quickly, but you also know that if you slow too quickly you might become a bug on the bumper of an 18 wheeler. The goal is to get to the shoulder as quickly as possible, but that's a problem when you cannot see the shoulder.

I was lucky. I found the shoulder and started to pull over, but I hit it hot. The bike got squirrely, but when I stopped I was still upright. There was nothing to do but wait for the rain to ease enough that I could get back on the road safely.

The storm only lasted only a few minutes and soon I was back on I-40 headed to Winslow. I could have followed parts of old Route 66, but the excitement in the rain had given me the yips and I just wanted to get where I was going safely.

When I got to Winslow, I checked in to the La Posada Hotel, which was the last of the famous Harvey House Hotels. It opened in 1930 at the start of the Great Depression and never prospered. It was closed to the public in 1957. The building was gutted, and it became offices for the Santa Fe Railway. In 1997, Allan Affeldt bought the hotel and restored it into a museum piece. It is a wonderful place.

I didn't have a reservation, so I went to the front desk hoping for the best. There was one guy ahead of me checking in. This guy had to be a lawyer or have *special needs* (maybe both). He was smallish and wore reading glasses held around his neck by a string. The receptionist gave him the usual paperwork and indicated the usual places to initial and sign. He would read parts of the paperwork through his glasses, then peer over them to ask questions.

Special needs guy: "Do I need to include my driver's license number?"

Receptionist: "No sir."

Special needs guy: "Where do I park?"

Receptionist: "In the parking lot."

Special needs guy: "When is check out time?"

Receptionist: "Tomorrow morning."

Special needs guy: "Blah, Blah, Blah?"

Receptionist (thinking to herself): "Good God, hasn't this guy ever checked into a hotel?"

Me (to myself): "Ahhhhhhhhhhhhhh!"

The receptionist finally got the guy checked in. My generally patient disposition saw me through the ordeal.

Ironically, the receptionist who had put up with Mr. Peepers was named Harmony. She found me a wonderful room with a king bed, a leather couch and a Jacuzzi. I checked in and found that the hotel had a great bar. So rather than standing on a corner in Winslow, Arizona, I opted to sit on a barstool. The bartender was obsequious (look it up Stevie Ray), but a pretty good guy. Two beers and one Knob Creek and soda later, I was in bed reading my Baldacci novel.

This is the story about my ride the day after I had been caught in the bad rain I talked about in the previous story. It's not as exciting as the last story, but it describes some must stop spots along Arizona's Route 66, including some of the sites where the movie Easy Rider *was filmed.*

Cratered in Arizona

THE MORNING I LEFT Winslow after being caught in some dangerous rain, I rode through Flagstaff, Arizona (I didn't forget Winona) to Kingman. Most of this ride is on I-40, but there are some fun Route 66 spots along the way.

The first is the Meteor Crater, which is about six miles off of I-40. It is 570 feet deep and a mile across. It was formed 50,000 years ago when a 60,000 ton meteor slammed into the countryside. It's impressive, but you should decide whether it's worth the time. It is on private property and there is a hefty fee to get in. Visitors pass through a museum before getting to the crater. There is some interesting literature about its origin and the unsuccessful search for the nickel of which the meteor was thought to be made. Once at the crater there is a walkway around part of the perimeter, but you can't go into it.

Two Guns is the next stop. It was a tourist destination capitalizing on Canyon Diablo and the legend of Harry "Two Guns" Miller. The town originally was named Canyon Lodge but was renamed Two Guns after Miller killed a neighbor who was operating a business that competed with Miller's business. Miller pled self-defense and was acquitted even though the victim had been unarmed.

Two Guns is near the Canyon Diablo ghost town, which was founded in 1881. The main drag was named Hell Street, which had 14 saloons, 10 gambling houses, four whore houses and two dance halls. 🎵🎵🎵 *These are a few of my favorite things* 🎵🎵🎵. The first sheriff took office at 3:00 one afternoon and was killed by 8:00 that same night. There were five more sheriffs, and none lived more than a month.

The Twin Arrows are just a few miles past Two Guns. The trading post there opened in 1949 and the distinctive arrows were put up in 1954. They are made out of telephone poles and are 20 feet tall. There once was a restaurant, a curio shop and a gas station. It closed in 1998 and has deteriorated. There has been some restoration, and I had hoped that the newly opened Twin Arrows Navajo Casino would generate interest in reopening the trading post, but there doesn't seem to me much local enthusiasm for that.

Flagstaff is just past Twin Arrows, and it has lots of neat stuff, but on this trip I just rode through without stopping. I'll do a complete post on Flagstaff sometime. I once won a karaoke contest there.

Bellmont is the first town past Flagstaff. The Pine Breeze Inn is there. This is the motel from the movie *Easy Rider* from which Dennis Hopper and Peter Fonda were turned away when the proprietor turned the bright red "NO VACANCY" sign on as they rode up.

I watched *Easy Rider* a few months ago. I was 14 years old in 1969 when it came out and it seemed so cool. Watching it at 59 years old was a different deal. The whole thing consists of Dennis Hopper being drugged out (successfully) and Peter Fonda walking around trying to look cool (unsuccessfully). Then there is the young Jack Nicholson riding Bitch with a football helmet on. That also seemed cooler in 1969. At least the music still is great.

Anyway, the original NO VACANCY sign is in a museum inside the nearby Roadhouse Café, which is an interesting joint. They make you cook your own food. So, if you order a cheeseburger, they give you a hamburger patty, some cheese and a roll, and you have to cook it yourself at a communal gas fired grill. Salad and beans are free. It's an odd arrangement but it works OK.

After Bellmont is Williams, which like Flagstaff, is a story for another day. But then comes my favorite stretch of Route 66. It is nearly 160 miles of uninterrupted Old Road, almost all of which is out of sight of I-40. It starts just past Ash Fork and goes all the way to Topock, Arizona near the California line. Kingman is a bit past the halfway mark.

Stay tuned. That's the next blog.

Endnote: *I visited Twin Arrows in October 2022, and one of the Arrows had blown over a few days before my visit. There are political problems in getting the Arrow repaired because the site is on Hopi land, which makes the repair contingent on a survey to assure that no Hopi relics will be disturbed. The Arizona Route 66 Association is doing its best to get the restoration completed by the 100th anniversary of the commissioning of Route 66, which will be in 2026.*

This story does not describe any particular events. It is about my favorite stretch of Route 66. It's 165 miles of the original 1926 alignment of Route 66 that stays away from the Interstate Highway. The second half of the ride is over the Oatman Highway from Kingman, Arizona to Topock, Arizona at the border with California.

This is a ride for which no words can substitute for experience. If you can visit only one stretch of Route 66 this should be the one.

My Favorite Route 66 Ride

WESTERN ARIZONA OFFERS bikers one of the best rides in the United States. The ride is over 160 miles of original Route 66 in two distinct sections. The first half starts just west of Ash Fork at the Crookton Road Exit off of I-40 and ends in Kingman. The second half goes from Kingman over the Oatman Highway, which ends in Topock, AZ, near the California border.

Ash Fork to Kingman

The Ash fork to Kingman ride passes through half a dozen small towns, some of which still have thriving motels, restaurants and shops. The road winds through rolling hills, grasslands and valleys, as wells as evergreen forests. The fragrance reminds bikers why they are on two wheels instead of being in a cage. Almost the whole ride is outside the view of I-40. And as a bonus, much of the ride is in the High Desert that keeps things cool even in the summer months.

This is what motorcycle riding is all about.

The first town is Seligman, which is 20 miles down Crookton Road. There are a couple of sets of Burma Shave Signs along the way. These signs appeared along U.S. highways between 1925 and 1963. They were put up by the Burma-Vita Company to advertise their popular

Burma Shave brand of shaving brushes and shaving cream. Each set was a series of six small signs arranged 100 yards apart. The first five signs would include a Burma Shave pitch or give driving safety advice and the last would say "Burma Shave." An example might be: "*Train Approaching…… Whistle Squealing…… Stop…… Avoid that Run Down Feeling…… Burma Shave.*"

There are lots of cool shops in Seligman. There are a couple of decent motels and the "World Famous" Black Cat Bar, but the big destination is the Snow Cap Drive-In, which may be the most photographed burger joint on Route 66. It has been known for decades as a place where the owners play practical jokes on their customers. The only problem is that management sometimes focuses more on entertainment than on serving food. Service can be slooowwwww. Still, for folks not in a hurry it's worth the stop. It is closed during the winter months.

Peach Springs is the next town. It was founded in the 1880s as a railroad water station. There were 10 saloons, no churches and no schools. Later it had a roadhouse and a stagecoach line. In the 1930s there was a gas station and an auto court. All of that is gone. Today Peach Springs is a prosperous town with the headquarters of the Hualapai People (People of the tall pine).

The next town is Truxton. There is not much there except the newly restored Frontier Motel sign. There was a small café and lounge, but they are closed.

A small scene from *Easy Rider* in which Peter Fonda fixes a flat on his bike was filmed in Valentine, which is near Truxton.

The Hackberry Store was opened in 1934 as the Northside Grocery and Conoco Station. It closed in 1978 when I-40 bypassed Hackberry. In 1992, artist Bob Waldmire bought it and reopened the Hackberry Store as a tourist stop. Waldmire sold it to the current owners in 1992.

Today it is part museum and part store. There is a 1960's Corvette out front along with other vintage cars, trucks, signs, gas pumps and vending machines. Inside there are more displays, including an entire soda fountain (non-operational).

Kingman is 20 miles past Hackberry. It was the hometown of movie actor Andy Devine. He is the corpulent frog voiced actor who played the coach driver in the movie *Stagecoach*, and the sheriff in *The Man Who Shot Liberty Valance*. Everything in town is named for him.

But Kingman is a story for another day.

The Oatman Highway

The Oatman Highway is not just one of the most beautiful rides on Route 66; it is one of the most challenging. It starts on the west side of Kingman and passes through several small towns, including Cool Springs, Gold Road and Oatman before ending in Topock near the California border. The winding road has hairpin turns that once led to gold mines in Siltgreaves Pass. This is a dangerous ride. Don't go up there on a motorcycle unless you know what you are doing, and don't go up there at all in bad weather. Even a car might get washed away in a flash flood.

But if you are on a motorcycle in good weather and you know what you are doing, it's perhaps the best stretch of road on Route 66. When speed limit signs say 10 MPH you'd be wise to pay attention; *however*, you have to keep up your pace. The problem is that there are steep hills with sharp turns with no guardrails. If you try to stop on one of those hills in the middle of a turn you *will* fall over, and if you are too close to the edge, the fall might kill you.

The first stop is Cool Springs. It opened in the 1920s and by the 1930s there were eight cabins for rent and a restaurant specializing in sandwiches and chicken dinners. It suffered after I-40 bypassed the Oatman Highway, and it burned down in the 1960s. Today all that's left is a gift shop and museum built on the stone remnants of the original structure.

There is a functioning gold mine in Gold Road. The mine operated between 1902 and 1943. At its peak there were 400 residents. Although the mine has been reopened there never seems to be much going on.

Oatman was a mining town named for Olive Oatman, a young girl who was kidnapped and enslaved by the Yavapai Indians. She was sold to the Mojave Indians, who tattooed her face in the Mojave tradition. Olive was released in about 1855 near Oatman.

Oatman is where Clark Gable and Carol Lumbard went after they eloped. Gable loved the area and would go there to play poker with the miners. Depending on the state of repair, you can view the room in the Oatman Hotel where Gable and Lumbard stayed, but you can't stay in the hotel; it no longer rents rooms. But you can get a cold beer and a good lunch there. The bar has good food and it's the only air conditioned building for miles around.

The ride from Oatman to Topock is fun but not as severe as the ride up the other side of the Oatman Highway. Once there, you will be on the California border. The Old Arch Trails Bridge crosses the Colorado River into California. This bridge, which once was known as the Route 66 Bridge, was featured in the opening credits of *Easy Rider* and was in *The Grapes of Wrath*.

So ends my favorite ride on Route 66. The next ride is across the Mojave Desert to Rialto, California.

This story is about my ride from Williams, Arizona to Rialto, California on the same ride as in the previous two stories. I was riding to Rialto for my first stay at the wonderful Wigwam Motel, where every room is a Tee Pee. I could have saved a couple of hours by Taking I-40 out of Kingman and skipping the Oatman Highway. The Oatman Highway is beautiful, but it's a dangerous ride, and every time I'm out that way I wonder whether I should risk it. I couldn't help myself, and I went ahead and took the Oatman Highway on that cool morning. I met some folks that afternoon at the Wigwam who became long lasting friends.

Rialto Reality

A WEEK OR SO AGO I was in Kingman, Arizona headed to Rialto, California. It was going to be a hot ride across the Mojave Desert, so I left at 6:00 a.m. to get in as many miles as possible during the cool morning weather.

Kingman is the entrance to the Oatman Highway, which is my favorite stretch of Route 66. It's about 50 miles over the magnificent Siltgreaves Pass. There are several old mining towns along the way, including Oatman, which is where Clark Gable and Carol Lombard went when they eloped.

On the weekends Oatman is a busy tourist town. Visitors feed the wild donkeys who are the ancestors of the pack animals that miners used over a century ago.

On this trip I zipped through Oatman before eight o'clock on a Monday morning. There were no tourists and none of the businesses were open. Even the donkeys had fled town to forage for their food in the absence of humans to feed them. At the far edge of town, a lone coyote trotted across the road in front of me with his tongue hanging out and panting as he returned home from his evening's hunt.

As I expected, once I got out of the mountains and entered the Mojave Desert, it got very hot very quickly. The temperature there routinely exceeds 120°, and with the heat generated from the road surface, I suspect it gets to over 130° while on a motorcycle. The air feels thick and burns your nose and throat, like in a sauna.

This day was no different. I did whatever I could to keep myself hydrated and cool. I stopped at every opportunity to drink cold water. Before leaving each oasis, I filled the pockets of my motorcycle club vest with ice, which would melt well before I reached the next stop. I even made one stop for an hour to let the engine on my motorcycle cool off. Overheating in the middle of the desert could be fatal.

All of these stops made the ride more tolerable, but it added a couple of hours to the trip. So I didn't roll into Rialto until late in the afternoon. I had a reservation at the Wigwam Motel. This is the nicer of the two motels on Route 66 where each room is its own individual Tee Pee (the other is in Holbrook, Arizona). When I entered the office the owner told me to take a free bottle of water. I had just had some water, so I thanked the owner but declined the offer.

He said, "I'm a Route 66 professional and I can tell when a biker needs water." I replied that I was a Route 66 professional too and I just didn't need any water at that moment.

He kind of mocked me, but he changed his attitude when I showed him my book, *The Motorcycle Party Guide to Route 66*. He loved it and told me he wanted copies he could sell to his Motel guests. I'm working on that.

I met some interesting folks at the Wigwam. The first was Kumar Patel, whose family owns the place. Kumar is an animated guy who clearly enjoys meeting Route 66 travelers. He knows all the other nearby Route 66 business owners and is up to date on all the Route 66 current events. He told me he loves the bikers because they always arrive early and have a fun time relaxing by the Wigwam's pool.

Kumar introduced me to Bob Kikkert from Canada. Bob and his wife were visiting the Wigwam as part of a celebration of their 50th wedding anniversary.

In 2014, Bob and his son rode Route 66 from Chicago to Santa Monica. They spent two years planning their trip and spent six weeks on their ride. I asked Jim what his favorite attraction was, and although he could come up with a few, it was clear he was like me. It wasn't the roadside oddities that made Route 66 special to him; it was the road itself. He told me that he felt that Route 66 had gotten into his soul. He has kept up with many people he met along the way, and through those relationships, he feels he is part of Route 66.

Kumar also introduced me to a journalism student from China named Ling. She had flown from Shanghai to Los Angeles, rented a car, and spent 45 days driving to Chicago and back to gather information for a book she is writing about Route 66. I asked her why she decided on a Route 66 project as opposed to some other famous road, such as the Pacific Coast Highway. It was clear that she hadn't really heard of other significant U.S. highways. For Ling, Route 66 was the most famous road in the United States with lots of history about the American heartland.

A week after I met Ling I received a wonderful e-mail from her. She said, in part:

"I finally finished the solo tour on Route 66… The sights, sounds and experiences of the 'Road' were great and will remain a lifetime in memory, but the best aspect, by far, of my trip was the people I met along the way."

Clearly, she gets it.

Endnotes: I've been back to the Wigwam many times. Kumar no longer works there, but his family still owns and operates the place.

Ling completed her book and sent me a copy. It's written entirely in Chinese except the part about how we met at the Wigwam, which is in English. She also included a large color photo of my Route 66 MC logo, which you can see on the title page of this book.

Somehow, I never wrote a story about Mike "the Hooligan" Callighan. But I have to include him in this book because I've ridden more miles with Mike than anyone else. We once rode 1,550 miles from Houston to Washington, DC. in under 24 hours. That's an average of about 65 miles per hour for 24 straight hours, including stops. After I recorded my YouTube videos on riding Route 66 from Chicago to LA in 10 days, I decided to see whether it actually could be done. Well, the Hooligan and made that ride in 8½ days. He once rode through all of the lower 48 States in under 10 days. We have plenty of rides left in us.

The Places and People

These stories focus on places I've been and the people I've met on my motorcycle rides rather than on the rides themselves.

This is artist Lowell Davis and me on the porch of his home in Red Oak II, which is just outside of Carthage Missouri. He lives in the actual house in which Old West female outlaw Belle Starr lived. Lowell was a gentle man who discovered that the fame his artwork brought him, and the first class travel he once took to his art shows, did not give him the same good memories he had from the simpler travel he took throughout the country in his truck with his dog Hooker.

This story is about the first time I met Lowell Davis, who was a world famous artist from a small town near Carthage, Missouri. He turned out to be a kind, gentle man, who had left the life of a successful artist who spent all his time traveling first class to market his artworks in favor of a more rural lifestyle.

There Ain't no Memories in First Class

A FEW WEEKS AGO I stopped by Red Oak II, which is a piece of art in the form of a village created by Lowell Davis outside of Carthage, Missouri. It was a wonderful visit to a beautiful place with an interesting, gentle man.

Lowell Davis was born in 1937 on a farm outside of Carthage,. His father had a wondering spirit, and soon after Lowell was born, he sold the farm, packed up his family and moved west. The family roamed from place to place, and Lowell's father never bought another piece of property until Lowell was in the fifth grade.

The family eventually returned to Missouri, first moving to Red Oak, about 20 miles outside of Carthage, then later to nearby Rescue where Lowell's father ran a service station on Route 66. They finally landed in Carthage, were Lowell's dad bought a small gas station and store. The family lived in the back.

Lowell had in interest in art early on. He would get in trouble at school for doodling on his books. He had a neighbor who was an amateur watercolor artist who helped him along. He got a small oil painting set for Christmas when he was in the fifth grade, and immediately thought that oils would be his medium of choice. At that point, he surely never suspected he would not only create wonderful oil paintings, but he also would become a cartoonist and a master sculptor using clay, wood, metals, porcelain and any other medium he could find.

Perhaps the most significant help in Lowell's early years was his fifth grade teacher, Miss Metsker, who financed his art lessons with Nell

Esterly, Carthage's only art teacher. Lowell created several paintings for Miss Metsker over the next two years.

Before he moved on to another teacher's class he did a pastel chalk rendering of Andrew Jackson's home that covered an entire section of the blackboard. That work remained on the blackboard for the rest of Miss Metsker's teaching career.

Lowell took a respite from his art career while he was in the Air Force. After his discharge, he went back to Carthage and set up his own commercial art business in a studio next to the Boots Drive Inn. This was a restaurant and souvenir stand owned by the folks who owned the Boots Court (the Boots Drive Inn closed in 1970; it now is the Great Plains Credit Union).

One day he was looking out the window of his studio when a hot young woman "Buzzed the Boots" in a shiny red and white 1955 Buick. Although Lowell didn't know her name, he told a friend who was with him that he was going to marry her. Her name turned out to be Nancy, and he sure enough married her.

Lowell wound up working as a staff artist for a local company that produced post cards and similar works. He also did well freelancing and selling original works on a commission basis. Eventually, he was noticed by his employer's biggest customer, and he was offered a job in Dallas to head up that customer's art department.

He started off doing artwork for brochures. After a few years, he was asked to create a risqué cartoon book. It was a huge success, and Lowell was asked to produce a series of these cartoon books, which became the 10th bestselling magazine in the United States. He eventually did 250 covers for the magazine.

Lowell got tired of the cartoon business, and he turned to wildlife paintings. He then transitioned into wildlife sculptures.

He had an agent that was able to sell all the artwork he could produce. He was making a lot of money, but he hated living in Dallas. His dream was to buy and restore an old farm. The problem was Nancy liked Dallas and had no intention of leaving. They wound up getting divorced.

Lowell traveled the country to his art shows in his truck, called the Leapin' Lizard. Lowell went through a period of depression and moved home to Carthage. On his way home from a bender in Atlanta after a failed art show, he met a woman named Charlie on an airplane and they eventually were married.

Lowell had begun creating paintings and sculptures of farm animals. The sculptures were lovely, and Lowell developed a following of collectors of his works. Lowell and Charlie would travel to art shows together in a beat up Dodge Charlie's father had given them and they stayed in a beat up tent trailer Lowell's father had given them.

Business was good, and they eventually saved enough to buy the farm Lowell always had wanted. They plowed (I know, bad pun) all the money they made into restoring the farm. They also bought other buildings and had them transported to the farm for restoration. By the time they were done they had a fully working farm stocked with farm animals.

The successful restoration of the farm gave Lowell the idea to create Red Oak II.

Lowell believed that artists should not be limited to making artworks only from traditional media. Red Oak II was to be a village laid out as a work of art. He intended to buy and restore the buildings that would comprise his creation. Every building was to be a separate piece of art that would comprise Red Oak II.

The first building he bought was a Feed and Seed Store. The second was the Elmira County Schoolhouse. The third was the Red Oak General Store from the town in which Lowell had lived as a boy. Next was the Blacksmith Shop Lowell's grandfather had owned. Eventually a church, a diner, a train depot, a marshal's office and a host of other buildings were added. Lowell himself lives in the house in which female bandit Belle Starr was raised, and an addition to the house is an exact replica of the cabin in which Belle Starr died.

Over time, Lowell's relationship with the company that distributed his sculptures ended and his revenue stream ended with the relationship. Charlie tired of the country life and moved to Chicago to become an airline flight attendant. Lowell and Charlie divorced, and Lowell eventually met his third wife, Rose, while he was on a trip to the Philippines with his best friend.

I did not know any of this on the sunny afternoon in May that I visited Red Oak II. I had pictured it as a kind of museum that I would have to pay to enter. Instead, there was an open archway and I just drove in. There were a bunch of children and a few dogs playing, and I asked whether I needed permission to walk around. The children told me I was welcome, and I made friends with the dogs.

The village was set up around a loop along a gravel road. Most of the buildings were empty, but they all were well maintained. I looked inside most of them and went inside some others. Where it appeared that someone was living in a building I respected the owner's privacy. One of the first occupied buildings had a slight man sitting on the porch smoking a pipe.

I walked through the whole town, and when I finished the loop, the slight man I had seen was in his front yard near the road. He seemed a little shy, but at the same time appeared curious about me. I introduced myself and asked if he was Lowell Davis, and he told me he was. He was exceedingly friendly and he invited me into his home to chat.

There was not much room, but the surroundings were comfortable. I had not done much research about Red Oak II or Lowell before my visit, so I didn't have many good questions to ask. Fortunately, he was glad to tell me about his career and the creation of Red Oak II, so I mostly listened.

Things were not displayed as in a museum; rather they were placed around as would be expected in an artist's workshop. He had a lot of original paintings and prints, as well as original sculptures.

I had seen Lowell's sculpture of the Crapduster at a convenience store just outside of Carthage, Missouri. He showed me the cartoon book in which the Crapduster first appeared. The Crapduster is a bi-winged flying manure spreader being flown by a local businessman who Lowell though was full of…… well, you know.

We talked some about his artwork, but after I told Lowell that I had written a book about Route 66, he began to tell me how it had changed since his boyhood days in the 1930s. He missed the mom and pop restaurants and motels that had been replaced by national chains. He told me about folks he had known on Route 66 his whole life. Some were living and some were long gone. He seemed to enjoy the reminiscing, and I enjoyed listening.

A table in his living room displayed copies of his autobiography: *There Ain't no Memories in First Class*, and I bought a copy.

He told me that while he was selling millions of dollars of artwork, his distributor would fly him first class all over the country to art shows and they would put him up in five star hotels. He had found that the folks in the first class cabins of airplanes were disinclined to speak with each other, and the beautiful hotels in which he would stay were equally sterile. He literally found that there are no memories in first class, and he went back to traveling the country in the Leapin' Lizard. He also went back to staying at motels that had windows he could open.

He signed my copy of his book "To Sam on your visit to Red Oak II. Your friend, Lowell Davis – May 2015." Next to his signature, he drew a paw print in remembrance of his dog Hooker, who traveled the country with him.

I had to think of how right he was that there ain't no memories in first class. I spent a good bit of my legal career flying first class to cities on my way to conference rooms where I sometimes worked for days without leaving, and to hotels that I sometimes never saw.

At the time it was exciting and everything I wanted my life to be. However, looking back, I was either working my ass off on those flights or grabbing some sleep because the airplane was the only refuge from the pressures of my profession. I would have been the guy next to Lowell who would have been too preoccupied with work to strike up a conversation.

I now have ridden my motorcycle through all of the 48 contiguous states and have written a book about my travels along Route 66. I fully understand Lowell Davis's wonderful memories of traveling the byways of this country with Hooker and meeting wonderful people along the way. For me, Red Oak II is one of those wonderful places and Lowell Davis is one of those wonderful people.

Endnote: *Lowell Davis died at Red Oak II on November 2, 2020. He was 83. Red Oak II is still there, and Lowell's artworks are readily available on the Internet.*

This story is about a stop we made on the first day on Route 66 while filming my Pilot TV Show, Kicks on 66. My Deacons of Deadwood MC brother Justin "The Kid" Dossett, my videographer Greg Sitler and I had just had hot dogs at Henry's in Cicero, Illinois. After lunch we stopped in Joliet and met Dick Bartel from the Dick's on 66 Towing Company.

Dick's on 66

Don't get excited, ladies. It's a towing company.

The day before yesterday, Justin "The Kid" Dossett and I stopped at Dick's on 66 in Joliet, Illinois. Dick's is a towing company, but it also is a mini Route 66 museum featuring restored antique cars. The best of them is a police car that has been in many magazines, including *Hustler*, which did a photo spread (in every sense of the word).

We were lucky enough to meet Dick, who has been running his towing company since 1960. Dick is a colorful guy who has spent his whole life on Route 66. He is 75 years old, but he looks 20 years younger and acts 50 years younger. On Saturday nights, Dick races stock cars against the grand children of the friends he raced when he was a kid.

Dick told us that Route 66 through Joliet has changed very little over the years. All the homes in the neighborhood predate the commencement of Route 66, and most of those houses have been in the same families for generations. The Rich and Creamy ice cream stand about 200 yards from Dick's has been owned and operated by the same family for over 50 years. The biggest change was the repaving and widening of the roadway. It once was paved with bricks, and when the bricks were replaced with concrete, Dick gathered up a couple of pallets of the old bricks as keepsakes.

His foreign visitors often remark on how much freedom we have in the United States compared to other countries. They marvel that he is allowed to own guns. When I asked Dick how to find the site of the original Dairy Queen, which was in Joliet, he told me "I can't remember the names of my three ex-wives, let alone where the Dairy Queen was at!"

Dick says he gets 15,000 visitors a year, and we got the impression that he has taken the time to meet every one of them. Be sure to stop by Dick's on 66 when you go through Joliet.

Endnote: *Later that day we met up with "Captain" Kirk Lane and Rodney "King" Fields in Wilmington, Illinois, who joined our film crew. In Wilmington we met Rex the Freeze Dried Dog. I never wrote a blog about Rex, but you can find out about him in my book,* The Route 66 Party Guide. *You also can open* bit.ly/3JhMAwk *in your browser to see a video about Rex on my YouTube channel, Route 66 Party Guide.*

Unfortunately, Dick Bartel died in May 2001. But the towing company and all the Route 66 exhibits still are on display, and Dicks on 66 remains a must see attraction.

This is the story about the first time I met the members of the Iron Sleds MC in Nilwood, Illinois. It was during the filming of my Pilot TV Show, Kicks on 66. They came with us to a big party the Full Throttle Saloon in Carlinville, Illinois threw for us later that night. There were several bare breastesses sightings.

Meeting the Iron Sleds MC

A COUPLE OF DAYS AGO a few of my Deacons of Deadwood MC brothers and I rode to the Full Throttle Saloon in Carlinville, Illinois, to film footage for my project to produce a Pilot TV show about riding motorcycles on Route 66. On the way, we visited the Iron Sleds MC's clubhouse.

I had passed by the Iron Sleds' clubhouse many times and had done some research about them in connection with my book *The Motorcycle Party Guide to Route 66*. They have a web site that says they are a family oriented motorcycle club that was founded in 1976. I also found that they were not a 1%er club, which is the designation outlaw clubs use to show they are among the toughest 1% of all motorcycle clubs.

There is a lot of protocol involved in visiting a motorcycle club. The problem is that the protocol can be different depending on the MC being visited, and you never know just how things will go until the meeting occurs. If you are not careful, things can go bad quickly. We met someone in Springfield, Illinois, the night before who rides with the Iron Sleds and we had him call ahead to ask permission for us to stop by. It's never good to surprise an MC by showing up unannounced.

The next morning I got a call from the Iron Sled's president. He asked me questions about who I was, who the Deacons of Deadwood are and why we wanted to meet the Iron Sleds. I expected those kinds of questions because MCs always are careful about who they will meet. An MC that is not a 1%er club may have an affiliation with a 1%er club. In those cases, the MC will have suspicions that unknown people may

The Places and People

be undercover law enforcement officers seeking incriminating information about the MC or the 1%er MC they support. Even if there is no 1%er affiliation, an MC may worry about undercover law enforcement because local police often are convinced that all MCs are involved in illicit activity.

I must have answered the questions well because the Iron Sleds president told us they would be happy to meet us.

The Iron Sleds turned out to be great guys. In the MC world, everybody has a "Road Name" that is used among the MC members. It's not uncommon for MC members to not know the actual names of their members. Only the Road Name is used. So, when we arrived I introduced myself as Sambo, and introduced my Deacons brothers as "Captain Kirk," "The Kid" and "Rodney King," whose real name is Rodney Fields.

The Iron Sleds' president was named "Weed." He looked like Popeye with an eye patch. He's not called Weed because he smokes dope; he has survived cancer and a few motorcycle wrecks, making him harder to kill tan a weed. He has been president for 16 years.

The clubhouse was Spartan but clean. There was a bar and some pool tables. There also was a cage on a stage used for strippers. Weed explained that they didn't bring in strippers, but they never object when someone decides to get in the cage and put on a show. Of course, there were old motorcycle engines and parts everywhere. These were the remnants of bikes that Iron Sleds' members had wrecked.

The most striking feature of the clubhouse was a wall dedicated to their brothers who had died. There were pictures and small memorials to each one, and the ashes of many were inside motorcycle gas tanks attached to the wall. One of the brothers had been a stone mason, and his ashes were interred in a hollowed out brick. They explained that the wall served to keep the entire brotherhood together within the clubhouse.

We had a great visit and invited them to meet us at the Full Throttle later that night. They did, and that's another story. Stay tuned.

Endnote: *I've been back to the Iron Sleds' Clubhouse several times since this visit, including for their 45th anniversary celebration.*

The Full Throttle threw us a great party. Open bit.ly/3SU4PLa *in your browser to see a video about that party. Warning: this one's not for the faint of heart or your kiddies, so watch at your own risk.*

I've always liked bars. This one makes my Top 10 Route 66 Bars list, which you can find in my book The Route 66 Party Guide.

Johnnies Bar: An Inspiration for Jerome Kern

Johnnies Bar (shouldn't it be *Johnny's?*) has been serving St. James, Missouri, since 1960 when John Bullock rented a 1926 building and opened the bar. Before Johnnies opened, the building had housed a series of cafes, a liquor store, a grocery store and a Greyhound bus depot.

Johnnies is the kind of place I knew I would like before I walked in. There is a distinctive Stag Beer sign out front. A Notice on the front door lists about 20 people who have been banned from entry. I asked the bartender what you have to do to get banned, and she said, "Quite a lot, actually". She offered no other explanation, but one of the customers told me that fighting is the primary banning offense. There must be some rough chicks at Johnnies, because a third of those banned were women.

Despite the fights, Johnnies is a friendly place. It is a smoky old school bar with super-cheap prices ($3.50 for Wild Turkey). The walls and ceiling are nicotine stained. A few one dollar bills with the names of customers who wanted their visits to be remembered are stapled to the ceiling. *Everybody* smokes (except me). The most popular song on the Juke Box is *Smoke Gets in your Eyes*. If secondhand smoke really affects bystanders, you could contract lung cancer just by hanging around.

There are a lot of antiques, like an old cash register, old liquor bottles and decanters, hornet's nests, an arrowhead display and some old fiddles. Johnny once was asked if one of the fiddles was a Stradivarius. He answered, "If it ain't, then I'm out ten bucks!"

The crowd is eclectic. Many of the women had tattoos and piercings in their noses, lips or both. The bartender had a tattoo on her face. Still, Johnnies has a good old boy atmosphere, rather than a punk atmosphere.

Other than speed smoking, playing pool is the big thing at Johnnies. Everybody brings their own pool cue, so you would think the quality of play would be strong. I'll leave it at this: Fast Eddy Felson could retire after one night at Johnnies.

Johnnies was worth the visit. The friendliness of the people I met was inversely proportional to the quality of the pool play. I guess they either have banned all the fighters, or they were fighting somewhere else that night. I'm looking forward visiting again in a couple of weeks.

I stay in Cuba often because the wonderfully restored Wagon Wheel Motel is the oldest continuously operated motel on Route 66 and the Missouri Hick Bar B Q restaurant is one of my favorite restaurants on Route 66. Cuba is an authentic Route 66 destination, and it's worth exploring for a few hours even if you don't stay overnight.

Diplomatic Relations with Cuba

Cuba, Missouri is a pristine little town about 85 miles southwest of St. Louis. It calls itself "The Mural City" after the 12 murals throughout town celebrating Cuba's heritage. The first mural was commissioned by People's Bank in 2001 to celebrate its 100th anniversary. It depicts the Bank's first cashier and the town's first Model T Ford. The People's Bank mural was so popular that a local community beautification group commissioned 11 more murals that were created by local and nationally known artists. Those murals feature other noteworthy Cuba events, such as civil war battles, visits by Amelia Earhart and Harry Truman and an unauthorized depiction of Bette Davis.

The big site in Cuba is "The Four Way," which is a restored 1932 Phillips Station at the four way intersection of Route 66 and Highway 19. It has a mural with three panels, one of which celebrates the 75th Anniversary of the founding of the Missouri Highway Patrol. The other two panels feature The Four Way during the heyday of Route 66.

I stopped in Cuba to try the Wagon Wheel Motel, which has been in continuous operation for over 70 years. It is the oldest continuously operated motel on Route 66. The Wagon Wheel has been fully restored to look as it did when it opened, but modern amenities (like updated bathrooms and showers) have been added. The neon sign has been restored and the grounds are well kept. They don't have a restaurant, but nothing is more than five minutes away. They actively seek biker business, and there is a covered area reserved for bike parking.

The Wagon Wheel may be the nicest of the restored old motels on Route 66.

Cuba has a couple of good restaurants and bars. The Missouri Hick Bar B Q is a fairly new place (it's been there about 10 years) that has been built to look more rustic than it is. Still, it is nice with lots of wood.

I live in Texas, and Texans are proud of their Bar B Q (even though they smoke the wrong animal). The Missouri Hick would put some Texas places out of business. I ordered a small pulled pork sandwich and a half rack of ribs. I did not plan to eat it all. It was so good; I ate every bite. The Missouri Hick may well be the best Bar B Q I have ever had. I often stop in Cuba just to eat there.

Frisco's is the local steak house. Its bar dates to the early 20th century and the restaurant was added about 15 years ago. Although it's billed as a steak spot, it has many other offerings. It has a family atmosphere and is brightly lit, and the food and service are terrific. Plus, it is one of the only two bars in town that stays open late.

The Rose is the other late night bar. It is dark and bawdy. Cuba is a pretty tame town, but as biker spots go, the Rose may be the best.

The East End Bar also is good, and of Cuba's bars seems to get the largest crowd. Unfortunately, that crowd largely is young couples with the children who roam pretty free and get under foot. But, it's a friendly place with decent bar food and a juke box featuring Classic Rock.

So, Cuba is worth an over-night visit.

Endnote: *I hear that the owner of the Wagon Wheel wants to sell the place and retire. What a great investment that would be for a Route 66 romantic!*

This museum is in a building that predates the commissioning of Route 66. Every inch is stocked with antique motorcycles. It doesn't take long to tour and is worth a stop.

The Seaba Station Motorcycle Museum

A COUPLE OF WEEKS AGO I was traveling through Oklahoma filming interviews for the Pilot TV show I am producing about riding motorcycles on Route 66, and I stopped by the Seaba Station Motorcycle Museum in Wellston, Oklahoma. I had visited the museum several times, but on this trip I hoped to meet Jerry Ries or Gerald Tims, who are the founders and proprietors. Unfortunately, I was there on a Wednesday, which turned out to be the only day of the week that the museum is closed. But I was able to catch up with Jerry Ries by telephone a few days ago.

John and Alice Seaba built and opened the Seaba Station in 1921, which was five years before Route 66 was commissioned. They originally sold a gasoline called Nevr-Nox, which was produced by the Tulsa-based Mid-Continent Petroleum Corporation. In 1925, Mid-Continent bought six gas stations from Diamond Petroleum Co. Mid-Continent began marketing the DX brand of gasoline in 1933. The "D" stood for Diamond, and the "X" represented a secret anti-knock gasoline additive. DX gas stations were prominent throughout Oklahoma and on Route 66 until they were discontinued in the 1980s by Sunoco, which had become DX's parent corporation.

Eventually, John Seaba turned the gas station into a machine shop that rebuilt automobile engines and produced connecting rods for the government. In 1951, Seaba sold the business to Victor and Sue Briggs. The Briggs' sold the building to Sonny and Sue Preston in 1995, who spent years restoring the facility, and operated it as an antique shop until they sold it to Jerry Reis and Gerald Tims in 2007.

Jerry and Gerald met about 20 years ago when Jerry sold Gerald a motorcycle. They have been riding together ever since. Jerry was a teacher (now retired), and Gerald owns Precision Motorcycles in Oklahoma City. They each had some vintage motorcycles and a vision of putting them on public display. Jerry and Gerald worked on the idea for nearly a decade, and they explored several options on where to establish their museum, including building new space. When they found the Seaba Station they knew they had their venue.

They were not looking for something on Route 66 in particular; it just worked out that way. But once they decided on a Route 66 location, they embraced it. Jerry and Gerald spent two years restoring the building's façade to its original state, and The Seaba Station Motorcycle Museum opened in 2010. Since opening they have tried to find DX Station and other Route 66 artifacts to display. Thanks to Jerry and Gerald, Route 66 now has another restored building that has been in operation since before Route 66 was commissioned.

Jerry and Gerald own about 90% of the 120 motorcycles on display and the rest are on loan from others. The oldest bikes are a 1909 Triumph and a 1913 Pope Board Trainer. The Pope was designed for racing on board tracks. Pope manufactured bicycles beginning in 1878 and produced motorcycles from 1902 until 1918. They still sell bicycles under the Columbia name.

There are two motorcycles from the movie *Captain America*. They also have a 1997 Triumph Bonneville and a 1999 Excelsior Henderson, each of which still are in their shipping crates. There are not many Harley-Davidsons, although they have a 1942 Harley Flat Head military bike. There are dozens of classic racing and competition bikes.

The stone structure out back is unique. From the road, it looks like a storage building, but it's actually a two-seater out house that is original to the Seaba Station from when it opened in 1921. It is supposed to be one of the first out houses to have flushing toilets and running water. Today, all that's left is the building and the remnants of the toilets.

The Seaba Station gets visitors from all over the world. It is a stop on a couple of poker runs a month, and they host two swap meets a year. Their only funding is through the sale of t-shirts and Route 66 memorabilia, along with donations from their visitors.

Endnote: *Just down the road from the Seaba Station on your way to Arcadia and the Round Barn, keep on the lookout for the ruins of an old Route 66 gas station. Supposedly, the place once was used to print counterfeit $10 bills.*

John Hargrove has created a roadside attraction that would have been noteworthy during the heyday of Route 66 roadside attractions. But John is more interesting than his creations.

John Hargrove's OK County 66 Mini Museum

I RECENTLY VISITED John Hargrove at his OK County 66 Mini Museum. John has created replicas and representations of many Route 66 attractions, including Twin Arrows, the Blue Whale, the Wigwam Motel and the Cadillac Ranch. All of these are interesting displays, but John Hargrove himself is even more interesting.

John looks younger than his 70 years. He claims to be falling apart physically, but that is far from the case. He works out religiously. He is not particularly musclebound and not overly trim, but he is one of the most physically fit people you'll meet. Incredibly, he has run over 40 100-mile road races. His longest run was 139 miles. Those are not typos. John talks about those extreme races like it's something everybody does all the time. He doesn't lift weights and he eschews stretching exercises. Instead, he believes the key to fitness is good joint health and he does exercises designed to keep his joints supple and in good working order. He is an exceedingly cheerful guy with a spritely enthusiasm.

John is a retired airline mechanic who grew up on 23rd St. in Oklahoma City right on Route 66. After he retired, he bought some property about a mile from the Round Barn in Arcadia, Oklahoma, and started the OK County 66 Mini Museum, which opened in 2001. He started building replicas of well-known Route 66 attractions and other Route 66 themed displays. Some of them are outright bizarre. For instance, he has a Volkswagen beetle sticking out of the second floor of his building. Visitors can squeeze themselves into the driver's seat and peer out over the grounds like they are the bombardier in a WWII Flying Fortress.

There is a rebuilt 1930s gas station. He has a replica of a diner that looks much like the one in the Hackberry Store in Hackberry, Arizona.

There also is a drive-in movie theater. The bathroom is an indoor outhouse. The facility is filled with Route 66 era memorabilia including antique signs, model cars and old books and magazines.

Oddly enough, John has not been to most of the sites that he has memorialized. Although he has traveled on Route 66 through Oklahoma (much of it while participating in hundred mile runs), he has not seen much of Route 66 outside of that state.

Even though the OK County 66 Mini Museum has a Route 66 theme, there's much more to see. John's business card says that he is in the automobile upholstery business, but he can build or restore anything. The day I was there he was finishing the restoration of a model A Ford. He also has a replica of a 1934 Indianapolis 500 racecar on display. For the bikers, he has a trike he made out of a Chevy Malibu. There are two wheels in the front with one wheel and back, and the cockpit has the full Malibu dashboard. All you Spider riders just shut it down!

John Hargrove is living life large. He doesn't sell anything and there is no charge to roam around his facility. He has built everything in his museum and be builds only the displays he wants to build. He takes on only the restoration work that interests him.

The OK County 66 Mini Museum is just east of the Red Barn in Arcadia. If you are traveling east to west, it's on the right-hand side at the crest of a hill. Be alert because it's hard to see.

It is not always open. You can call at 405 396 2055 to see if John is in. Visiting in the afternoon is your best bet. If the gate is open he's there.

By the way, if you take a left out of John's property and go about a mile, look to the right for an old marker that looks like a sawed off telephone pole. It marks the entrance to an older alignment of Route 66. For a brief and worthwhile adventure, take the right hand turn and follow it back to the main road.

Endnote: *I first met John and wrote this story in September 2016. I visited him again in October 2022, and he hasn't lost a step. John's museum does not have set hours of operation, but if the gate is open when you pass by be sure to stop in to visit him.*

The Blue Whale is one of the top five must see Route 66 roadside attractions, and when you get there, you'll be delighted to find that its every bit as grand as advertised. I was lucky enough to happen across Blaine Davis on one of my visits. His father Hugh built it as a birthday present for his wife Zelta. Blaine was glad to share his memories of this wonderful place.

A Visit with Blaine Davis at the Blue Whale

Last week I had the pleasure of interviewing Blaine Davis, whose family built and owns the Blue Whale in Catoosa, Oklahoma. It was a rare chance to get some inside skinny on the creation of this wonderful site.

Blaine Davis is the son of Hugh and Zelta Davis, who owned and operated the Blue Whale and the adjacent ARK for over 40 years. Hugh and Zelta also were the brother and sister in law of Chief Wolf Robe Hunt, who was a full blooded Acoma Indian renowned as a silversmith and as a painter of Indian art.

The Davis family bought 40 acres along the old Route 66 in 1952. Hugh Davis and Wolf Robe Hunt opened Wolf Robe's Indian Trading Post, which was the first business in the area. Route 66 was a paved two lane road that passed by the front of the Trading Post.

In 1955, a team of surveyors showed up to map the expansion of Route 66 into a four lane road, which was being realigned to go through the Davis's property. To build the new road, the government tore down three houses and destroyed a mature orchard on the property. The new road opened in 1959, and for a while, both the old and newer alignments of Route 66 were in use.

The new road was only about 100 yards from the old road, but it reconfigured the Davis's land. Route 66 now passed in back of the Trading Post and bisected the Davis's property. They took advantage of the new alignment by moving the front door of the Trading Post to be next to the new road. They also started developing the property on

The Places and People

the other side of Route 66, making the Davis's the only folks to own businesses on both sides of the new four lane highway.

The first business he built opposite the Trading Post was Zelta's Alligator Ranch, which featured live alligators. Later the Ranch was expanded to include other animals with which children could interact, and the name was changed to Nature's Acres. It became a popular petting zoo designed for children's birthday parties and similar events.

Hugh and Zelta began construction of the ARK in the late 1960s. ARK is an acronym for Animal Reptile Kingdom, and it became the office and gift shop for Nature's Acres. It was a two story structure shaped like a boat that was not completely enclosed, so it was subject to damage from the weather.

When the four-lane Route 66 reconfigured the Davis's land, a pond that was on that land was expanded. Local folks had been swimming in the pond for years, and Hugh decided to develop that part of the property. So in 1970, Hugh began construction of the Blue Whale as a birthday gift for Zelta. Hugh designed and supervised construction of the Whale, which is made of concrete and steel. It opened in 1972 and remained a popular swimming hole and adjunct to the Nature's Acres for years. *Time Magazine* rated it as one of the top 50 Roadside Attractions in the United States.

As time passed, Catoosa residents increasingly were building back yard swimming pools, and the birthday parties that used to be at the Blue Whale and Nature's Acres were moved to those back yard pools. By 1988, the Davis's base of support had eroded. They closed the Blue Whale and Nature's Acres then retired.

Today, the Davis's no longer own the Trading Post, but the building is still there. It now is called the Arrowhead Trading Post, but the business housed there is an automotive repair shop. About a half a mile of the old Route 66 that passed by the original front door of the Trading Post still is accessible and is worth exploring.

The structure that served as the original entrance to the Alligator Ranch still was standing in 2014, but it since has been torn town.

The ARK became dilapidated. The second floor collapsed and much of the wood in the structure has rotted. However, in the past six months, the ARK has been cleaned up and there are proposals to restore the building and operate a business from there.

As for the Blue Whale, after the Davis's retired the property was vandalized and was in disrepair. The overgrowth was so severe the Blue Whale could not be seen from the road, which was only 30 yards away. Finally in 1995, Blaine and some other Catoosa residents started to restore things. A little more is cleared every year and the Blue Whale again is a popular Route 66 attraction that gets visitors from all over the world.

Endnote: *This story was written in 2015. Since then the City of Catoosa purchased the property and significant restoration is planned, including a 1.2 mile, 12 foot wide "View Trail to the Blue Whale," that will connect Catoosa's Roger Berry Sports Complex to the Blue Whale. A series of hiking trails around the site also is planned.*

This story is about a ride on which my friend Ken Becker took me one afternoon to show me a long abandoned section of the original 1926 alignment of Route 66. Ken grew up near Weatherford, Oklahoma, and spent his youth along Old Route 66. He was there before I-40 was completed and bypassed Route 66. So, when he and his friends would ride to Amarillo to party, they took Route 66.

Ken knows everything there is to know about this stretch of Route 66, and I always learn something new when I ride with him.

The Road Not Taken

A FEW DAYS AGO I was traveling through Oklahoma on my way to Jackson Hole, Wyoming, and I stopped to visit my friend Kenneth Becker, who grew up on Oklahoma's Route 66. Kenneth has been exploring Route 66 his whole life and he always has interesting bits of information and stories about raising hell, drinking beer and doing all the imprudent kinds of things guys do when they are young. On this day, Kenneth took me to a few of his old hide-outs along some now abandoned portions of Route 66.

He started by showing me the "new" alignment between El Reno and Hydro. Construction of this 18 mile paved road began in 1930, and when completed in 1934, it bypassed the dirt road that went through Calumet, Geary and Bridgeport, all of which were on the original 1926 alignment.

I have always taken the original route through Calumet when passing through this part of Oklahoma, so getting to see the new road was a treat. There are no sites of note, but it is a wonderful ride. It is rural, hilly and picturesque. It still has the original concrete pavement, which is in great shape. It ends at the Cherokee Trading Post at I-40 Exit 108.

There is no sign marking this route, but it is easy to find. When traveling west on Old Route 66 from El Reno, instead of going right at the junction with Highway 270 into Calumet, go straight.

Like me, Kenneth Becker is an explorer and a historian. He's taken me to climb La Bajada Hill near Santa Fe and has taken me over many now abandoned portions of Route 66 in Oklahoma. He even knew Lucille Hammons, who ran Lucille's Roadhouse outside of Weatherford, Oklahoma on the 1926 alignment of Route 66.

From the Cherokee Trading Post we headed to the ruins of the Key Bridge.

The Key Bridge was a privately owned suspension toll bridge across the South Canadian River at Bridgeport, Oklahoma. It was built in 1921 by Oklahoma City businessman George Key. The toll was $1.00 for cars and $1.50 for trucks. The state of Oklahoma bought the bridge in 1930 and eliminated the toll.

The Key Bridge was bypassed in 1933 when the William H. Murray Bridge opened. This is the same "Pony Bridge" that you saw near the base of Bridgeport Hill. Bridges of this type are called Pony Bridges because their structural spans look like galloping ponies. There are many Pony Bridges along Route 66, but this is the longest, at over 4,000 feet in length and with 38 Pony spans.

With the opening of the Pony Bridge, the Key Bridge did not get much use, and it eventually was torn down for scrap. All that's left of the Key Bridge are the standards that held it up, and they are hard to spot without looking carefully. Still, its fun to visit these forgotten spots, and there's no telling what you might find. Kenneth carries a silver dollar he found a few decades ago laying on the ground near the Key Bridge.

After visiting the Key Bridge, we headed to the casino in Hinton, Oklahoma. All beer; no whiskey (what's that about?). Nonetheless, it had been a wonderful afternoon of seeing new places with an old friend.

Exploring long abandoned roads somehow has defined the second half of my life. *Two roads diverged in a wood, and I – I took the one less traveled by. And that has made all the difference.*

Endnote: *To get to the Key Bridge, go right out of the Cherokee Trading Post parking lot, go two miles and take the first left. You will be back on Old Route 66. Go for another two miles across Bridgeport Hill to a Stop sign at Highway 8. Turn left. A few hundred yards away you will see the 1933 "Pony Bridge" on a newer alignment of Route 66, but you will not go over that bridge. Instead, go 100 yards, and take an immediate right onto CR 1010, which is a gravel road. Stay on CR 1010 and veer onto CR 2630/2620. Follow to the left onto CR 1000, which is Old Route 66.*

This dirt portion of Route 66 has never been paved. Follow it for 2.5 miles to the ruins of the Key Bridge, which will be on your left. Keep a look out because it's hard to see.

The Places and People

I'm showing may age with the title to this story. It's about a service station and motor court that Lucille Hammons operated along the 1926 alignment of Route 66 for 59 years. The title is from the beginning of the Little Richard's song "Lucille," which has nothing to do with Route 66. Little Richard was very big in early Rock and Roll. With lyrics like "Good golly Miss Molly, sure like to bone," he was one of the guys who 1950's radio stations banned to protect the nation's youth.

None of this has anything to do with Lucille's Roadhouse; I just thought the title would be fun.

My friend Kenneth Becker, who is featured in the previous story, knew Lucille. To see a video with Ken telling about his recollections of Lucille, open bit.ly/3KXO4P5 *in your browser.*

No trip across Route 66 is complete without a stop at Lucille's. So, I hope you enjoy this story and I encourage you to watch the video.

Loo – Ceil, Please Come Back Where You Belong

ABOUT TEN DAYS AGO I was visiting Lucille's Rodhouse between Hydro and Weatherford, Oklahoma, to film some interviews for the Pilot TV show I'm producing about riding motorcycles on Route 66. I was with my friend Kenneth Becker who grew up near there and who had known Lucille.

Lucille's was a filling station built by Carl Ditmore in 1929. W. O. Waldrop bought it in 1934 and named it the "Provine Service Station." Waldrop later added a five-room motor court. He sold the business to Lucille and Carl Hamons in 1941. After the Hamons bought it, the place was known as the "Hamons Court," "Hamons Service Station" and finally "Lucille's."

During WWII, traffic along Route 66 declined significantly and Carl became a long distance trucker to earn extra money. Lucille was left to run the place alone. Many of the Okies and Arkies passing through on their way west were broke. Lucille would feed and give them gas in exchange for appliances and other possessions they might have. Sometimes she would take their broken down cars in trade and the travelers would catch a bus going west. Other times, she just fed the folks for free. Lucille became known as the "Mother of the Mother Road."

When I-40 replaced Route 66 between Hydro and Weatherford, direct access to Lucille's was cut off and she lost much of her service station business. The motel also closed. Undaunted, Lucille installed coolers and sold beer to the residents of Weatherford, which was a dry town. That's when my friend Kenneth came in.

Kenneth was 19 years old in 1970. The drinking laws in Oklahoma were peculiar. Men could drink beer in a beer joint or buy beer to go at age 21. Women couldn't drink beer in a beer joint until they were 21, but they could buy it to go at age 18. When I asked Kenneth about liquor (as opposed to beer) sales, he just laughed and said, "This is Oklahoma!"

Kenneth says Lucille was a slim 5'2" tall woman who had a permed hair style of the day. Kenneth said she looked like a grandmother, which she was, and was friendly to all her customers. She was there all the time and lived in an apartment above the store.

Lucille's wasn't a bar or beer joint. It did not get big crowds and it was not a bawdy place. It was more of a convenience store that had beer and a pool table. Many locals, including students from Southwest Oklahoma State University, went there primarily because Lucille would sell them beer even though they were not 21 years old.

In the early 1970s, nobody thought of Lucille's as a special place. Moreover, Route 66 was not thought of as a special road. There was no Route 66 tourism, at least not of the sort we have today, which consists largely of explorers seeking out the relics of a bygone era. That's because the era was not yet bygone. I-40 had not been completed, and Route 66 still was the local road used to travel through the string of still prosperous towns across central Oklahoma and the Texas Panhandle. Kenneth remembers I-40 as a bigger tourist draw than Route 66 because in 1970 nobody in central Oklahoma had ever been on a "superhighway."

Lucille sold her last gallon of gasoline in 1986 and the station became a souvenir shop. She continued to operate the place for another 14 years until she died at age 85 on August 18, 2000. It was a 59 year run. The Hamons family donated the original "Hamons Court" sign to the Smithsonian in 2003, and it is displayed there in an exhibit called "America on the Move."

Locals tell me that the original Lucille's now is owned by a large company that has opened a new restaurant in Weatherford called Lucille's Roadhouse. The owners have spruced up the original Lucille's and have rebuilt the old motel building. The word is that the owners of the new place won't open the old place from fear of losing business to the old place. They should. If the old place was open to sell only souvenirs and cold drinks, every Route 66 traveler would stop for a few minutes, get the t-shirt and a beer, and be on their way, maybe even to the new restaurant. However, even if the current owners never reopen the original Lucille's, everyone should thank them for preserving this small piece of American history.

Route 66 has many museums. On one of my trips west, I visited four of the best of them in a single day. I hope my story about these museums are good enough to encourage you to visit them yourself.

Four Museums

During my ride between Weatherford, Oklahoma and Tucumcari, New Mexico, I visited four museums. Three were in Oklahoma and one was in Texas.

The Thomas P. Stafford Air and Space Museum in Weatherford is not Route 66 themed, but it is worth a visit. General Stafford commanded Apollo 10, which was the second mission to orbit the moon and the first to fly a lunar module there. Although he orbited the moon he did not walk on it.

Many of the exhibits are replicas, like reproductions of a lunar landing module, the Spirit of Louis and the Wright Brothers airplane. However, there are many exhibits of authentic fighter planes and rocket engines. The coolest exhibit is the actual control console used during the Apollo missions. Compared to modern equipment it looks like a toy; but it got our astronauts to the moon and back.

The Oklahoma 66 Museum is just down the road in Clinton, Oklahoma. The Museum offers a self-guided tour through six decades of Route 66 history. There are vintage cars and exhibits focusing on road construction, transportation, lodging, restaurants, curio shops, attractions and other artifacts. Outside is a tiny diner that operated in Shamrock Texas from 1956 to 1964. Dozens of those diners were manufactured by the Valentine Manufacturing Company of Wichita Kansas.

Trade Winds Motel across the street from the Museum was a favorite of Elvis Presley. He liked Room 215, and you can stay there too.

In Elk City, Oklahoma I visited the National Route 66 Museum. Outside, it has the world's largest Route 66 shield. Inside, there are exhibits about each of the eight states through which Route 66 passes. There are displays of quirky roadside attractions and antique cars. There also are many interactive hands-on displays, such as a "Drive" down Route 66 in a 1955 pink Cadillac, and you can watch a black and white movie in a replica drive-in theater while sitting in a classic Chevy Impala.

The last Museum I visited was the Texas Route 66 Museum in McLean, Texas, which was the last Texas Route 66 town to be bypassed by I-40. It is one of my favorite museums on Route 66. It is not as slick as the museums in Clinton and Elk City, but it has an authenticity that the others somehow lack.

The Texas Route 66 Museum claims to be the first Route 66 Museum in the United States. It was opened in 1991 by Delbert Trew, who says he knows all of the exhibits are real because he stole them himself. Although this Museum is small, it has some interesting exhibits including the original statue of the steer that was at the Big Texan Steak House in Amarillo, and a giant yellow snake that was outside the Regal Reptile Ranch in Alanreed. There also is the interior of an actual diner that once operated along Route 66.

The Devil's Rope Museum is in the same building. It is much bigger than the Route 66 Museum. It has exhibits about the history of barbed wire and photos of Texas ranches and their operation. This might sound like pretty mundane stuff, but it is fascinating, especially for people interested in cowboy history.

Finally, this building has a small gallery about the Dust Bowl. This gallery is in one small room and is the smallest of the three exhibits, but in its own way, it is the most interesting. It consists mostly of photos of people and farms from the McLean area along with commentary about what it was like to live through the Dust Bowl. The photos of poor families are haunting, especially the photos of the children, who seem playful and happy despite their poverty. The pictures of dust storms are surreal.

If you don't stop at this museum you'll be missing something special.

Endnote: *If you want to see the Trade Winds Motel in Clinton that Elvis liked so much you better get over there soon. It's being torn down and being replaced by a Clinton school system administration building.*

My stories usually stay away from politics. This one is an exception.

What Happens in Vega Stays in Vega

I drove to Jackson Hole, Wyoming, recently to attend the celebration of my friend Paul Hartman's life. I met Paul and his wife Marilyn nearly 30 years ago. They were a couple of hippies who met in Hawaii and got married, then moved to Jackson. They started out working as a waiter and waitress (oops, I guess now I'd have to call them "servers") at a steak house. They later bought some hat making equipment and opened the Jackson Hole Hat Company. Paul would make the hats and Marilyn would sell them. I could tell a hundred stories about these wonderful people. Paul will be missed.

On the way to Jackson I stopped in Vega, Texas. Vega is famous for Dot's Mini Museum, which is a small room of Route 66 and other nostalgic collectables. I've never found it open, but it's still considered a Route 66 classic.

Vega also has the 1947 Vega Motel. Despite internet postings claiming the Vega Motel is going strong, it is closed, but the sign and facility are in decent condition.

The Boot Hill Saloon is open, and I often stop in Vega just to go there. It is relatively new construction, but it looks like something out of the 1890s. There is a tall tin ceiling, solid wood bar and red velvet upholstery on the chairs at the tables. The menu is ambitious for a town the size of Vega, but they pull it off well. It is a biker destination on the weekends. I give this place a rating of 3½ shot glasses out of five.

I got up before sunrise (no, I'm not making that up) to get headed to Jackson. I saw hundreds of red lights flashing in the distance simultaneously. Turns out they were lights on the wind turbines that have been constructed across the Texas desert.

The environmental do-gooders love wind power. They claim that it provides a cheap renewable source of energy. Well, it turns out it's not so cheap and not so reliable (ask Boone Pickens). Plus, they kill hundreds of thousands of birds each year. No doubt we have lost millions of spotted owls, California condors, and golden cheeked warblers to these propellers of death. I guess the renewable energy do-gooders trump the wildlife do-gooders.

The environmentalist crowd loves to regulate everyone's lifestyles except their own. So, they push for the required use of mass transit while they travel to environmental conferences in their private jets; they call for the regulation of water use in drought stricken California while they water the grass on their multi-acre mansions; and they push for wind turbines in places like Vega. But you never see them near rich folks' homes. Ted Kennedy was apoplectic when wind turbines were proposed within view of his Hyannis Port mansion. Typical. A "liberal" is someone who will give you the shirt off of someone else's back.

People from places like Vega see beauty in the land in which their families have lived for generations. These windmills have not only defiled the Texas skyline. They now pollute the wonderful night sky with those red lights peering down like Satan's eyes burning across the stars. Very sad.

Endnote: *The Boot Hill Saloon has not survived. But if you are in Vega try Roosters Restaurant. It's a locals hang out but the locals are very friendly. The food is great. They don't have a bar, but you can get cold beer and excellent Margaritas.*

Tucumcari always has been one of my favorite Route 66 towns because of all the vintage neon signs. I first visited Tucumcari in the early 1990s, and most of the old signs were lit at night even if the businesses being advertised had closed. It was easy to imagine what Tucumcari once looked like.

This story gives some history about how Tucumcari was founded and focuses on the Blue Swallow Motel and how it fared after I-40 bypassed the town.

Tucumcari Tonight

I rode across the Texas Panhandle to Tucumcari, New Mexico a few days ago to stay at the Blue Swallow Motel.

This ride goes through the heart of the Llano Estacado, which in Spanish means the "Staked Plains." It got its name when Spanish conquistador Francisco Coronado traveled through it in search of the Lost City of Gold. The area was so broad and devoid of landmarks that he had to put stakes in the ground to find his way out.

I've gone through the Llano Estacado many times, both in summer and winter. In the summer it is very hot and in the winter it is very cold. This ride was no exception. The weather was fairly cool until I got west of Amarillo. After that, the temperature was over 100 degrees. Fortunately, Tucumcari is only about 125 miles west of Amarillo, so the ride was not too severe.

Tucumcari once was a crossroads of commerce and was one of the busiest towns on Route 66. It was founded in 1901 when the Chicago, Rock Island and Pacific Railroad built a construction camp there called Ragtown. It later was called Six Gun Siding because of the frequent gunfights. Still later, it was called Douglas. Finally in 1908 it was renamed Tucumcari after nearby Tucumcari Mountain. Legend has it that the mountain got its name from two lovers: Tucom and Kari, who died tragic deaths during a dispute between their parents' leadership of a band of Apaches.

For years, Tucumcari had been notable for the many billboards advertising "Tucumcari Tonight" to attract visitors to its dozens of motels and restaurants. Until recently, Tucumcari had one of the best remaining sets of neon signs along Route 66. Although many of the businesses had closed, the signs had been kept in good repair and they were a show when lit up at night. When I got to Tucumcari on this trip, I found he signs were still there, but most of them were not lit. Another brick of Route 66 crumbling. Too bad.

The sign at the Blue Swallow Motel has survived. This bright blue sign with a swallow that flaps its neon wings and boasts of the Motel's *100% Refrigerated Air* is perhaps most photographed motel sign on Route 66.

The Motel originally was called The Blue Swallow Court after the motor court style of construction in which each room had its own attached garage. It was opened in 1939 or 1940 by Ted Jones, who operated it until 1958 when Mr. Jones and his wife died. Lillian Redman and her husband bought and modernized it, including adding the now famous neon sign in 1960.

The Redman's loved their business and enjoyed meeting their customers. Lillian once said: "I have been traveling the highway in my heart with whoever stops here for the night."

When Tucumcari was bypassed by I-40, all of the businesses in Tucumcari suffered, including the Blue Swallow. Lillian said: "When Route 66 was closed to the majority of traffic and the other highway came in, I felt just like I had lost a friend. Some of us stuck it out and are still here on Route 66."

Lillian sold the Motel in the late 1990s and the new owners performed extensive renovations. In 2011, Cameron and Jessica Mueller took over and they have restored the motel to its original motor court style, including a working rotary telephone in each room. It is not fancy, and it is not luxurious, but it is an authentic Route 66 experience. The rooms are well appointed with new mattresses, high thread count sheets and plush towels. It reminds me of the newly restored Boots Court in Carthage, Missouri, except unlike the Boots, the Blue Swallow has televisions and Wi-Fi.

The Blue Swallow used to be closed in the winter months, but it now is open year round.

It's worth going out of your way to stay at the Blue Swallow but be sure to get a reservation. It's always full.

Endnote: *Since writing this story, even more of the vintage signs are dark. But Tucumcari still is a great town to visit. While I think the Blue Swallow is the best place to stay, the Safari Motel across the street has been renovated and is a good second choice. If they both are booked, try the Roadrunner Lodge Motel. And there's always the Pow Wow, which has the Lizard Lounge attached. It's the best bar and one of the best restaurants in town.*

If you read the previous story you found that my first exploration of La Bajada Hill was not too successful. This story is about actually climbing from the base to the summit and back down with my friend Kenneth Becker.

Climbing La Bajada Hill

THE ORIGINAL 1926 ALIGNMENT of Route 66 went through Santa Fe, NM. To get there, travelers had to traverse La Bajada Hill over a volcanic rock roadway that was part of the original El Camino Real de Tierra Adaptor. That was the primary commercial corridor between Mexico City and Santa Fe from 1598 until 1881, when a railroad to Santa Fe was completed. Still, the road up La Bajada Hill remained in use, and between 1903 and 1926 it was the primary automobile route into Santa Fe when it was New Mexico's Highway 1. During that time, laborers from New Mexican prisons built retaining walls to shore up the road to prevent erosion.

The original climb was less than 1.5 miles long, but it had 23 hairpin turns and was so steep that cars with gravity fed fuel lines had to go up in reverse so gas could reach the engines. To help with that problem, a less severe road was built in 1932 to service the ascent of the Hill, and the original alignment was used for the descent.

The road up La Bajada Hill was abandoned in 1937 when Route 66 was realigned to bypass Santa Fe. Since then it has not been maintained and it is in severe disrepair. That makes it all the more fun to explore.

My friend Kenneth Becker and I had long thought about driving up La Bajada Hill, but we decided we should hike it first to see if it was passable in an automobile. We went in the morning to avoid the hot afternoon weather in the New Mexico desert.

Ken works in the oil field and knows how to prepare for an exploration of this sort. He wore a wide brimmed cowboy hat to protect his face from the sun, blue jeans and sturdy steel toed boots. I'm a city boy and was less prepared. I wore a cap I bought at the Blue Swallow Motel in Tucumcari, cotton Izod shorts with navy blue lobsters on them and my Duluth Trading Company Mocs.

The access to the Hill from the bottom is so narrow it looks more like a path than a road. But just a few dozen yards past the entrance it opens up. The weather was reasonably cool, and the hiking was pretty easy. Ken scampered up like a mountain goat. I dragged my corpulent ass up the Hill with a minimum of huffing and puffing.

We soon found that La Bajada Hill is the fire ant capitol of the world. We also saw some collared lizards and some horn toads. They were the only species of critters we saw during the entire hike, which was good, because it looked like rattle snake territory to me. We also saw yellow and purple blooms on the cactuses that grow out of the rocks on the sides of the road and out of the retaining walls.

About halfway up the road splits. The right fork is the 1932 alignment that became the ascent to the top of the Hill. The left fork is the original 1926 alignment that became the descent.

We took the right hand fork. The grade became more severe the farther we went up, but overall it appeared to us that an ATV with good knobby tires could make it. However, when we approached the summit, the road became rough and had so many large boulders that it appeared un-passable. We plodded on and in a few minutes we had reached the top.

I was pretty happy with my performance. I had not held Kenneth up too badly and I had avoided a heart attack. We rested a while and headed across country for the ¾ mile walk to the beginning of the descent. There is no road connecting the 1926 and 1932 alignments, but our path was easy to find because we could see the electric power towers that lined the 1926 alignment. The view across the plains was spectacular, and we reflected that centuries of travelers had seen that same vista from the summit of La Bajada Hill.

The downhill road was in much better condition than on the uphill side. I had less huffing and puffing, but it still was a difficult hike because the footing was so unstable.

About a quarter of a mile past the fork dividing the ascending and descending routes, Kenneth saw an ancient petroglyph. We knew that petroglyphs were supposed to exist along the road, but we just flat out missed them on our uphill climb. There were a dozen or more of them and we took the time to explore and take plenty of photos. These petroglyphs were created between 1300 and 1600 A.D. The people who left these markings knew their meanings and they could communicate using them, but their meanings are lost today.

We started back down and a few hundred yards from the bottom of the Hill we encountered a guy from Africa who was driving up. He stopped to chat and told us that he drives his Land Rover up the Hill all the time. We told him about the petroglyphs, which he had never seen. So, we got to trade information with a fellow explorer. A few minutes later we were back to our starting point.

The round trip hike was about 3.8 miles long and took about two hours to complete. It had been all we had hoped for, and we were glad to find that it is passable in an automobile. That will be an adventure for another day.

A couple of words of caution: This is a fun hike, and I can't wait to try it in an ATV. But it's dangerous. If you become incapacitated on La Bajada Hill, you could die up there. Don't try it alone. If you get in trouble there likely will not be any help available. The road surface is unstable, and it would be easy to fall and break an ankle or incur some other serious injury. Stay hydrated. Be sure you are in reasonably good physical condition. Other than these worries, have fun!

Endnote: *Some of the petroglyphs on La Bajada Hill recently were desecrated and the Native Americans on whose reservation La Bajada Hill passes have made it less accessible. Some of the gates on the fences that block the road that used to be unlocked now are locked. If you want to explore La Bajada Hill, please be careful and respectful.*

This story is from a day during the longest motorcycle I have ever taken. My friend Elza Smith and I stopped in Grants, New Mexico, and happened across the first annual Fire and Ice Motorcycle Rally that Grants hosted for several years.

Fire Melts the Ice in Grants

FIFTEEN YEARS AGO I was with my friend Elza Smith on the longest motorcycle ride I have ever taken. We went over 8,500 miles from Houston to Vancouver and back *via* the Canadian Rockies (including the ride between Bamph and Jasper; Glacier National Park in Montana; Deadwood, South Dakota for the Sturgis Back Hills Rally; over Bear Tooth Pass in Montana into Yellowstone; Jackson Hole, Wyoming; Santa Fe, New Mexico and back to Houston.

Three or four days into our ride we rolled into Grants. New Mexico, where the first Fire n' Ice Motorcycle Rally was underway. It was full of Bandidos but seemed pretty peaceful. The 15th Fire n' Ice Rally was held about two months ago. It looks like it was the last one.

Two days after the 2015 Rally concluded, Rally Chairman Manuel Vasquez stated that the Rally went as expected and that "… nothing major took place… minus some over-intoxicated individuals that had to be escorted out…" He further said that although about 150 Bandidos showed up, they never entered the entertainment tent and in general they were well behaved. Vasquez said he had spoken with all of the vendors, and they reported that they had made lots of money, and that although final numbers were not in, the Rally appeared to have been a financial success.

The Mayor of Grants, its Police Chief and its City Council did not concur.

The Chief of Police said that there is a spike in crime, including many fights, each year during the Rally. That year at one point there were 11 different fight calls happening simultaneously, and a police officer was injured while trying to break up a fight. The Chief said that on the Saturday of the Rally he saw at least 150 people carrying guns and over 60 on Sunday. Compounding the trouble, the Bandidos reportedly forced all other motorcycle club members to remove their Colors.

One City Council Member said "We are asking for trouble. It's a numbers game. Eventually something will explode."

Mayor Martin Hicks said "Every year the bikers come to town crime goes up… Bullets don't discriminate. I don't want that many guns here…" He said that the Rally had been on rocky financial footing for years, that he knows his town pretty well and that the folks who live in Grants were fed up with the Rally.

Not everybody agrees. Most of the postings on the Rally's social media outlets support the Rally and the revenue it generates for Grants. Local newspaper accounts contained positive testimony from people who work in Grants. There were over 1,300 motel rooms booked. One woman made enough money during the Rally to buy her children's school supplies. Another woman used her earnings to get badly needed dental implants.

On August 10, the City Council met and considered discontinuing support for the Rally. After a spirited debate, the Council voted 2-2 not to approve the Fire n' Ice Rally in 2016, and the Mayor cast the tie breaking vote against support. The Mayor suggests a Route 66 car show or some similar "family friendly" event to replace the Rally.

This is a dicey situation. It could not have been much of a surprise to the Grants City Council that a bike rally likely would attract a rowdy element. They must have known that the Bandidos would be there, and that since New Mexico has an "open carry" law that allows the open carrying of firearms without a permit, many of the Bandidos would be armed. Nonetheless, other than a few fights and some drunkenness, there does not appear to have been much in the way of lawlessness.

On the other hand, the Bandidos forcing "civilians" to remove their motorcycle vests must have been a cause for concern, especially considering the gun fight between the Bandidos and the Cossacks in Waco, Texas earlier this year in which several bikers were killed and many more were wounded.

Kip Attaway never has had a job other than as a singer – songwriter. I met him in Jackson, Wyoming in 1986, when he was playing at the Million Dollar Cowboy Bar. He writes love songs, like *"It's Hard to Say I Love You While You're Sitting on my Face,"* or changes the words to existing songs to parody them. I've sung his songs at many Karoke contests, and I either get cut off and kicked out or I win. He's played for the Deacons of Deadwood MC so many times that we made him our first Honorary Member. He cut up his patch and made a Deacons of Deadwood Guitar that he uses in all his shows. I don't think Kip has ever been on a motorcycle, but he's one of the only guys I know that puts on more miles traveling the Country more than me.

Williams, Arizona, is my favorite Route 66 town. Here's a story about a night I spent in Williams after checking into, and then out of, a motel in Seligman.

Wild Times in Williams

This is a story from a year or so ago when I was riding through Arizona on Route 66. The story comes to mind because I recently turned 60 (although my liver probably turned about 75).

I was in the Black Cat Bar in Seligman, Arizona. It's supposed to be "World Famous" and a big biker place in the summer. Well, it was Deadsville USA that night, so I checked out of my motel and headed over to Williams to hit some of their World Famous bars.

Williams reminds me of how Jackson Hole, Wyoming was 25 years ago. The two towns don't look like each other, but they have the same feel. The air is fresh and crisp at night, and the stars are on top of you. Folks walk around in cowboy hats and boots that are not costumes. They listen to real country music. Stuff like Ray Price, George Jones, Johnny Cash and guys like that. Not the modern Nashville country sound that Merle Haggard famously said was "… nothing but bad rock and roll."

Williams was the last Route 66 town bypassed by an Interstate highway. Unlike many old Route 66 towns, Williams has continued to thrive, probably because of its cool night air and its proximity to the Grand Canyon. The Grand Canyon Railroad takes passengers out of Williams to the Canyon in restored antique coaches.

I went to the World Famous Canyon Club, which is one of my favorite bars on Route 66. They were having a party for someone on his 72nd birthday. I got there just in time to help sing the song to him.

After a while, he came up to me and said, "How's it going Old Timer!" That really didn't make my day. I was nearly 15 years younger than the guy. But, I took his salutation with grace and bought each of us a shot of Wild Turkey. Guys out west don't drink pussy shooters.

They were having Karaoke that night, and after about ten Turkey and sodas, I signed up to sing *Downtown*, Petula Clark's hit song from the 60s, only I used Kip Attaway's revised lyrics.

🎵🎵🎵 *Out there where some wino slept;*
There's some puke and some dog shit,
So watch where you step, when you're
Down-Town, out where the perverts are;
Down-Town, you can hock your guitar;
Down-Town, somebody's following you 🎵🎵🎵

For those of you who have not heard Kip's version, you know it gets worse.

I usually get unplugged when I sing Kip's *Downtown*. You can find Kip and me singing it on YouTube.

Well, this time, everybody got a hoot out of it, so I signed up to sing Kip's version of *Lookin' for Love in All the Wrong Places*, which is even worse: "*… Lookin' for love in all the wrong places; shooting up drugs and sittin' on faces…*".

After I got away with that one, I sang my own lyrics to Paul Anka's tune *Oh, Please Stay with Me, Diana*. It's so bad Kip says he's going to record it. It will take him to a new career low.

A good time was had by all. I passed out a bunch of route66mc.com Koozies and got some new registrations to the site out of it.

After the Karaoke was over, I scooted over to the World Famous Sultana Bar, which has the oldest liquor license in Arizona. It has been in continuous operation since 1906, which is six years before Arizona became a state. It ran Bar Girls for at least 20 years after that kind of thing was outlawed in Arizona.

The atmosphere is Old West. There is an original tin ceiling that must be 15 feet high. There are lots of stuffed trophies, including a moose, a mountain lion a caribou and an elk.

Fortunately, they had plenty of Turkey over there too. I closed the place down at 2:30 or so and made it back to my room safely.

Endnote: *I had taken the precaution of having some Coca Cola on hand to guard against a possible late night dry mouth attack, like the one I had in St. Louis when I needed a late night Coke, and in going to the vending machine down the hall locked myself out of my hotel room, naked, without my room key and not remembering my room number.*

Victorville has a strong Route 66 heritage and one of the best of the Route 66 museums. I don't know much about the town, but I always have a feeling that it's a dangerous place to be if you don't know where to go. Maybe it's because of the first time I stayed there. Here is that story.

Victor Victoriaville

A WHILE AGO I VISITED Victorville, California. On the way into town I stopped into the California Route 66 Museum in Old Town Victorville. It is in a 5,000 square foot facility that once was a Red Rooster Restaurant. There are three viewing rooms that feature rotating displays of memorabilia the Museum owns as well as borrowed exhibits. There are lots of photos of Victorville and the surrounding area depicting old Route 66 days. It doesn't take long to visit and it's worth the stop.

After visiting the Museum I headed into town. I found that Victorville is, well, *different*.

I planned to stay at the New Corral Motel because it had a newly restored neon sign of a rearing palomino. I stopped for gas on the way and asked the counter guy about the New Corral and he euphemistically told me that I could "meet some chicks" there.

Not to be deterred, I stopped into a local bar and asked about the New Corral, and the bartender told me that if I stayed there I "… definitely would get robbed."

So much for the New Corral.

I wound up staying at the Green Tree Inn, which was pretty worn, but overall OK. I didn't meet any chicks, but at least I didn't get robbed.

I Googled local bars, and it looked to me like a place called T-Zers was the place to go. I asked the clerk in the lobby of the Green Tree for directions, and she told me it was closed because two people were murdered there a couple of weeks previously.

So much for T-Zers.

I looked for another bar and wound up at Johnnie Fingers Sports Bar. It turned out to be a pretty friendly place, with cold beer and good drinks.

While I was there, someone came in and asked if anybody had heard any news about a shooting at the Dollar General. The bartender said she had heard about it an hour or so previously. The guys who had come in said that the police had just arrived at the crime scene.

Like I said, Victorville is *different!*

I left Victorville the next morning and headed toward LA. I stopped off at Bono's Deli in Fontana, which has been around since 1936. It is owned by Sonny's cousin. I had saved up my appetite because I wanted to have lunch there. Unfortunately, it was closed, and I was told they would reopen in six months.

So much for lunch.

I was supposed to pick up a chick who was flying in to LAX to meet me and ride back to Houston. She canceled on me, so after I hit LA, I turned around and headed back east.

So much for the chick.

I wound up back in Victorville at the same hotel I had stayed in the previous night. I was ready for a cold beer, and the lady at the check-in desk directed me to the hotel bar. When I got there I found a crowd leaving who told me that they had been waiting for an hour for the bar to open, and that they had given up.

So much for a cold beer.

So, I decided to write this Blog before going to the Iron Hog Saloon in Oro Grande. It's a hard core old school biker place about ten miles east of Victorville that I had wanted to try for a long time. While I was riding there I thought that with my recent luck it probably had burned down.

Stay tuned for an account of my adventure at the Iron Hog!

This story is about my first visit to the Iron Hog Saloon in Oro Grande, California. I was the day after my first visit to Victorville. I've been to the Iron Hog several times since this visit, but it's hit or miss as to whether it's open. When it is, it's an Old School biker experience.

The Iron Hog Saloon

I was in Victorville, California, for a second day after I went to LA and turned around to head back east. It was a peaceful night in Victorville. There were no murders and I didn't get robbed. The newscasts in most towns report on murders, robberies and other crimes because those are newsworthy events. In Victorville, it's newsworthy when there aren't any murders, robberies or other crimes.

I was heading to the Iron Hog Saloon in Oro Grande, which is a biker bar about six miles outside of Victorville. When I got there, it turned out the place had been closed for about a year, but they were getting ready for a Grand Opening the next day.

I met the owner, John Lambrech, who was nice enough to sit down with me and drink some bourbon and tell me about the history of the Iron Hog and his plans for its future.

We chatted amidst the bustle of workers setting up furniture, cleaning up and generally readying for the opening. There was a table of women making homemade hard candies that were to be given to the customers. I popped one in my mouth and told one of the confectioners that the candy tasted funny.

She replied that it was because it was laced with pot. I spit it out. No more of that for me!

John and I settled in, and he told me that over the years, the facility had been a farm equipment dealership, a roadhouse, a biker bar, a strip club and a house of ill repute. John was getting ready to reopen the place with at least three of the five previous businesses, and farm equipment wasn't one of them.

The Iron Hog started off as a Butterfield stage stop in the 1890s. It was the only trading post in the area. In the 1930s it was rebuilt into its current configuration and became a roadhouse that was frequented by Roy Rogers and Dale Evans, who carved their initials into the bar.

The movies *Easy Rider*, *Poker Run* and *Erin Brockovich* all had scenes filmed at the Iron Hog. It also has hosted first-rate entertainers like Johnny Cash.

The food is fantastic, but if you don't want to order from the restaurant, there are bar-b-q pits where you can cook your own steak.

The place sits on three acres of land, so there is plenty of room for outdoor concerts, bike rallies, poker runs and other events. There is a paved parking lot with video security reserved for bikes. There is a campground with facilities for RVs.

The Iron Hog is no place to take the kiddies. It is an old school biker spot that admits all colors. They have loud live music, a full bar and cold beer. There are stripper poles with dancers that the Iron Hog employs, and customers are permitted to try them out too. Breastesses abound!

I had to travel east the next morning, so I didn't get to go to the Grand Opening, but the fun I had the night before told me that I was going to miss a good time. I'll be back to Oro Grande in about a month and I'll be sure to stop by the Iron Hog. I have the feeling that I'll have plenty to report.

Sonny Bono, of Sonny and Cher fame, was from a family that has owned a restaurant in Fontana, California since 1936. Sonny's cousin Joe had owned it for years, but it had been closed when I had first met Joe four years before writing this story. I met him again on a later Route 66 ride, and he was gracious enough to give me an interview. This is that story.

A Visit with Joe Bono

A COUPLE WEEKS AGO I was nearly 4,000 miles into a motorcycle ride that took me from Houston to the start of Route 66 in Chicago, then from Chicago to Rialto, California. Before heading home, I wanted to see if I could find Joe Bono, whose family has owned Bono's Deli on Route 66 in Fontana since 1936. Kumar Patel, whose family owns the Wigwam Motel in Rialto, told me Joe lived in a house behind the Deli, and if Joe was home he was sure Joe would be glad to speak with me.

I had met Joe nearly four years previously when I was gathering information for my book, *The Motorcycle Party Guide to Route 66*. The Deli was closed at that time but was scheduled to reopen in six months. I thought Joe had told me he was Sonny Bono's uncle, but after some digging, I realized that could not be so, since Sonny and Joe were born in the same year. Both Sonny's and Joe's parents immigrated to California from Sicily in the early 20th century. They must be cousins.

I called the Deli's phone number but got an answering machine with a computer generated salutation. I rode the eight miles to Fontana anyway hoping I could find Joe. When I arrived, I looked inside the Deli, but no one was there. So I walked around back to the house, and it looked empty too. I was about to leave when a familiar man shuffled around the corner. It was Joe and he said he would be glad to speak with me.

Joe told me his parents came to Fontana from Sicily in the 1920s to raise wine grapes on 200 acres of vineyards they had purchased. It was a hard life filled with hard work and mixed success.

In 1936, Joe's mother opened an orange-shaped juice stand to augment the family's income. There were many similar stands along California's Route 66, but the Bono's was the first on the south side of the road. It is one of only six remaining orange-shaped juice stands in California.

As traffic along Route 66 increased, Joe's mother expanded her business to include the current Deli. She catered to the growing Italian community in and around Fontana and carried Italian foods that otherwise were unavailable in the area.

Route 66 travelers were an important part of the Deli's business. Joe's mother would stay open until at least 11:00 at night to serve those customers. She also was a generous woman who understood the hardships of her day. Joe remembers that his mother often would feed large families in need without charge.

When Joe became old enough, he would work in the vineyards with his family. He would drive the trucks on which his father and older relatives would load the harvest. Those trucks still are parked at the edge of the Bono's now abandoned vineyard across the road from the Deli.

Joe speaks of his mother with reverence. She had only a fourth grade education, but she started and ran her Deli, and put her four children through college. Joe graduated from USC and the USC Law School. He later worked in the San Bernardino County District Attorney's office for ten years.

Fontana has seen dramatic changes along Route 66. Joe tells me that at one time there were over 50 vineyards around Fontana and now there are none. There also was a prosperous citrus industry with orange, lemon and grapefruit groves. They too are gone. Housing has replaced them.

Joe is a sweet and gentle man. He said he hopes to reopen the Deli in the next month or so, but he had told me that four years ago. He tells me that his biggest impediment is navigating through the government bureaucracy for the necessary permits. But I get the feeling that what he really needs is the support his family provided throughout his life. He says, "I sure could use my mother right now."

Endnote: *In the summer before the Pandemic I visited Bono's and found that Joe had died and someone outside of the Bono family had bought it. It had been reopened as an Italian restaurant with a full menu rather than just being a deli. The place was full, the food was good and I had a great time.*

I went back after the Pandemic. It hadn't survived.

Route 66 History

These are stories about the creation of Route 66; historical events that occurred on Route 66 after it was commissioned in 1926; and events that happened in the towns and on the roads that were incorporated into Route 66 before it was commissioned.

This is a quick history about how Route 66 came into existence in the first quarter of the 20th century through the vision of Cyrus Avery.

A Brief History of Route 66

The Beginning

The creation of Route 66 began in the early 1920s through the vision and diligence of Cyrus Avery. Avery was born in Pennsylvania in 1871. His family moved to Missouri in 1881. Avery moved to Oklahoma City in 1904 then to Tulsa in 1907. He set up a realty firm and a coal company and speculated in oil and gas leases. Avery became one of the most prominent citizens of Tulsa.

Cyrus Avery was an early devotee of establishing a national roadway system. In 1921, he became president of the Associated Highways Association of America. In 1923, he was appointed Commissioner Highways of the State of Oklahoma. In 1924, he was a member of the American Association of State Highway Officials, which at its national meeting in San Francisco, requested that the Secretary of Agriculture underwrite and establish a comprehensive interstate road system. Avery was appointed to act as a consulting highway specialist to the Bureau of Better Roads, which was to create the beginnings of that system.

In 1925, Avery and others began selecting existing roads that would be part of the national highway system. Road clubs around the United States lobbied to have portions of their local roads included. A portion of a transcontinental highway that went from Chicago to St Louis and Kansas, west through Tulsa and Oklahoma City, and over the National Old Trails became the genesis of Route 66.

Before the establishment of the national highway system most roads had local names. The national highway commissioners decided to give roads across state lines shield shaped signs signifying that they were US highways or circular signs for state roads. The most prominent roads were to be designated by two digit numbers ending in zero. Politicians from Missouri and Illinois lobbied for the Chicago to Los Angeles route to be designated Route 60. They lost, and in early 1926 these politicians selected the designation Route 66 for the national highway from Chicago to Los Angeles.

On November 11, 1926, federal and state highway officials approved the interstate routes for all 48 states, and Route 66 came into existence.

In February 1927, the first meeting of the National US 66 Highway Association was held in Tulsa, and the Association adopted the name The Main Street of America for Route 66.

Expansion and Early Improvements

In 1920, the United States had approximately 3,000,000 miles of roadway, but only 36,000 miles had all weather surfaces suitable for automobiles. When Route 66 was commissioned, only about 800 miles of Route 66 were paved. The National US 66 Highway Association, along with corresponding state Route 66 associations, set out to get the entire route paved and promoted as the most direct route between the Great Lakes and Pacific coast.

It took until 1937 to pave the entire route. Advertising campaigns in national and local magazines and newspapers promoted the use of Route 66 and the businesses along the way. These advertising efforts were successful and the towns and businesses along Route 66 prospered.

The Great Depression and WWII

The stock market crashed, and the Great Depression began in 1929, only three years after Route 66 was established. Then, in the 1930s severe droughts in the mid-west and southwest caused the Dust Bowl. Tens of thousands were displaced. Route 66 became the highway that poor dirt farmers hoped would take them to a land of better opportunity. It became romanticized as the road to progress that resulted in the greatest westward migration in the country's history.

Route 66 came on hard times during World War II. Gas and tire rationing made long distance automobile travel impractical. In addition, production of new cars was suspended during World War II, making the purchase of reliable vehicles difficult. Most of the traffic along Route 66 consisted of military convoys and job seekers heading to large manufacturing plants in California.

A second migration along Route 66 occurred immediately after World War II as veterans followed Route 66 eastward from California to their pre-war homes, and families moved westward to California in search of better jobs. Travelers began to use Jack Rittenhouse's 1946 *A Guidebook to Highway 66* to steer them along. 1946 also was the year Nat King Cole released Bobby Troup's tune *Get Your Kicks on Route 66*.

In 1952, the Main Street of America Highway Association (formerly the Highway 66 Association) traveled Route 66 from the Chain of Rocks Bridge, which connected Illinois and Missouri, to Santa Monica, California, and dedicated Route 66 as the Will Rogers Highway.

The Boom Years, the Decline and the Renaissance

Route 66 was at its peak in the post-World War II boom years of the 1950s. However, in 1954 President Eisenhower established the President's Advisory Committee on a National Highway Program. This Committee designed what became our modern national highway system. Super-highways like I-55, I-44, I-40 and I-15 simply bypassed much of Route 66, which no longer could handle the increasing westward traffic.

In addition, the 1965 Highway Beautification Act prohibited billboards along these super-highways, making it difficult for businesses in the bypassed towns to advertise. Although some Route 66 towns continued to prosper, the replacement of Route 66 with super-highways and the prohibition of billboard advertising led to an inevitable deterioration of the road that was once The Main Street of America.

Route 66 was decommissioned in 1984. The US Highway 66 Association tried to get the interstate highways over which Route 66 once passed to be designated as Route 66, but it was unsuccessful in those efforts. I-66 now designates a road connecting I-84 in Virginia with Washington DC.

A little more of the old Route 66 seems to disappear every year. Restaurants, motels and old roadside attractions that survived on Route 66 for decades seem to slip away, especially in the west.

But even as some is lost, Route 66 is an organic organism with new life being created each year. Active state and local Route 66 Associations have had success in preserving and restoring traditional Route 66 attractions. Even more exciting is the rise of private businesses that either are resurrecting older Route 66 businesses and roadside attractions or creating new ones guaranteed to dazzle today's Route 66 explorers.

If you've never traveled Route 66, you'll find joy in experiencing both the traditional and newer Route 66 attractions for the first time. If you are a veteran Route 66 traveler, you'll be heartened to find your old friend is doing just fine.

This story is a partial list of motels, stores, restaurants, bars, buildings and other places that were on Route 66 when it was commissioned in 1926 that still remain today. I don't go into much history here, but the story can serve as a quick checklist of old places you might want to see as you explore Route 66 in the 21st century.

Happy 90th Birthday Route 66!

1926. Prohibition was half over but the Country was awash in bootleg booze. The stock market crash that would bring the Great Depression was as unthinkable as shuttering the speakeasies. Flappers were flapping away to songs like Five Foot Two. Eyes of Blue. *Yep, the 1920s were roaring, and life was grand.*

In 1926, Walt Disney Studios and NBC were formed. John Baird made the first public demonstration of the television. Thomas Edison declared that Americans always would like silent films better than talkies, *no doubt because he didn't have the patent on* talkies. *Satchel Page made his debut in the Negro Southern League and Harry Houdini stayed underwater in a coffin for an hour and thirty one minutes. Robert Goddard launched the first liquid fuel rocket.*

On November 11, 1926, Route 66 was established as the first National Highway to go from Chicago all the way to the West Coast. Ninety years later, folks are still getting kicks on Route 66.

Introduction to *Kicks on Route 66* – a video by Sam Allen

Lots has been written about how Route 66 has changed since its zenith in the post-WWII era. However, 90 years after its commencement, it's also fun to reflect on what was on Route 66 on the day it was born.

When Route 66 was commissioned on November 11, 2016, only about 600 of its 2,500 mile roadway between Chicago and Los Angeles was paved. Route 66 largely was rural, and much of it remains rural. It's still possible to get a feel for what Route 66 must have been like in 1926.

The roads connecting the Route 66 towns in Central Illinois; the original route through St. Louis to Gray Summit in Missouri; the road from Commerce to Weatherford, Oklahoma; the 1926 alignment through Santa Fe, New Mexico; the 160 miles from just outside of Ash Fork through Seligman, Kingman and Oatman to Topock, Arizona; and the old road from Chambless to Newberry Springs, California all are portions of Route 66 that are much the same today as they were in 1926, except back then they were dirt roads. When traveling these roads today, it's easy to imagine driving with your family in an unreliable Model T Ford, on an unlit dirt road in the middle of the night, hoping to make it safely to shelter that likely was scores of miles away.

I'm surprised at how many original Route 66 sites remain, especially since the boom of motels, service stations and other supporting businesses had not begun, and almost none of the eye popping roadside attractions for which Route 66 became famous had been built.

I have focused on highlights rather than trying to identify all of the survivors. I hope I have hit most of your favorites.

Illinois

Lou Mitchell's Restaurant. Today, Route 66 starts on Adams St. in Chicago, which is one way heading out of town. But in 1926, it started on Jackson Avenue, which ran two ways. A mile or so down Jackson Avenue, Lou Mitchell's Restaurant had been in operation for a year. Lou Mitchell's still is a traditional spot to get breakfast before beginning the journey from Chicago to Santa Monica. You won't leave hungry.

The Castle Car Wash. The Castle Car Wash on Ogden Avenue in Cicero was opened in 1925 as a gas station. Over the years, it also has been a car wash, a garage, and several other businesses. It has been closed for over two decades, but it still looks great and remains a must see Route 66 attraction. Rumors of a restoration are kicking around, but nothing concrete appears to have emerged.

The White Fence Farm. Romeoville's White Fence Farm was serving chicken dinners when Route 66 was established. The place is huge, with several dining rooms and museums featuring antique cars and motorcycles. I don't think the menu has changed since the opening day. You get all the pickled beets, creamy bean salad and cottage cheese you can eat (which for me is none). They don't have a bar, but you can order a Martini, Rob Roy, Old Fashioned, Manhattan or Whiskey Sour. They claim to have the best chicken dinners in the world, and although I can't speak for the world, I can't remember having chicken better than the White Fence Farm serves.

The Rialto Square Theater; Joliet Prison. Joliet has a couple of original Route 66 classics. The Rialto Square Theater opened in 1926. Joliet Prison, the namesake of "Joliet Jake" Blues, opened in 1858. It held Leopold and Loeb, who murdered 14-year old Robert Franks in 1924 in an attempt to commit the perfect crime. Clarence Darrow defended them, successfully arguing that they should not get the death penalty because they were nuts.

Old Log Cabin Inn. The Old Log Cabin Inn in Pontiac opened in 1926 and Route 66 ran right by the front entrance. When Route 66 was realigned to pass in back of the restaurant, the owners jacked the whole thing up and spun it around so the road still would pass by the front.

Funk's Grove. The folks at Funks Grove have been making maple sirup from the sap of over 3,000 maple trees since 1891, and they were open for business when Route 66 opened.

The Place Just off 66. Deck's Drug Store opened in Girard in 1894. Three generations of Deck's operated it until 2001. In 2007 the original soda fountain was reopened as Doc's Soda Shop. It since has been resold and now is a lunch place called The Place Just Off 66.

Marvel Theater. Carlinville's Marvel Theater opened in 1920 but burned in 1926. It was reopened in 1928. The current marquis is from the 1960s.

The Loomis House Hotel. The Loomis House Hotel in Carlinville opened in 1870. It was a house of ill repute into the 20th century.

The Luna Café. The Luna Café opened in 1924 in Mitchell with booze, broads and gambling. Its distinctive neon sign, which has been restored, features a cocktail glass with a bright red cherry inside. Lighting the cherry signaled customers that prostitutes were on hand.

Ariston Café. The Ariston Café originally opened in Carlinville in 1924, but it later was moved to Litchfield.

Soulsby Station. Mt. Olive's Soulsby Station opened in 1926 and was the oldest Route 66 gas station.

Missouri

Sherman's Grave. Civil War General William Tecumseh Sherman made his last march in 1891 when he was buried in the Calvary Cemetery in St. Louis, which was (and remains) on Route 66.

Gillioz Theater. Springfield's Gillioz Theater opened in 1926 to serve Route 66 travelers. It has a wonderful marquis.

Springfield Town Square. Springfield's Town Square was the site of a famous shoot-out in which Wild Bill Hickok killed Dave Tut in an argument over a poker game, a woman and a watch. There is a marker on the Square on the site of the shoot-out.

Spencer Ghost Town. Spencer was founded in the 1870s and was a ghost town by 1912. It was revitalized when Route 66 opened in 1926 but was a ghost town again after Route 66 was realigned. It is remarkably well preserved, and the road through town is one of only four stretches of original Route 66 that has never been repaved or widened.

Kansas

Eisler's Store. Eisler's Store opened in Riverton in 1925. Today it's called Nelson's Old Riverton Store. It sells groceries and souvenirs and serves sandwiches.

Brush Creek Bridge. The Brush Creek Bridge near Baxter Springs was built in 1923. It is the last remaining Marsh Arch Bridge on Route 66. These bridges were designed by James "Barney" Marsh and were known as "Rainbow Bridges" because of their distinctive rainbow-shaped arches.

Little Brick Inn. Baxter Springs has been known as the toughest town in Kansas, the first cow town in Kansas and the most robbed town in Kansas. Today's Little Brick Inn originally was a bank that Jesse James robbed.

Oklahoma

Commerce Marathon Station. Commerce, Oklahoma, which was Mickey Mantle's hometown had a Marathon Station that opened in 1925. It has been a Dairy King Drive-In since 1980.

Ribbon Road. The first portion of the nine foot wide Ribbon Road between Miami and Afton was opened in 1921 and a second portion opened in 1922. It was incorporated into Route 66 in 1926. A small passable portion still exists.

Tulsa. Tulsa is a Route 66 museum in its own right. Going east to west, Tulsa's Route 66 is on 11th Street. It is rural on the outskirts today, and it must have been exceptionally rural in 1926. There are lots of old buildings that no doubt were there when Route 66 opened. Someone should do one of those "Yesterday and Today" type books.

11th Street Bridge. In 1926, travelers would leave Tulsa over the 1915 11th Street Bridge. It was renamed the Cyrus Avery Memorial Bridge. The bridge was bypassed in 1978, and it is immediately adjacent to the current bridge leaving Tulsa.

Seaba Station. The Seaba Station in Warwick opened as a gas station in 1921. Today it is a motorcycle museum. It has the original stone two-holer out house out back.

Threatt's Store. Threatt's Grocery and Gas Station was opened in Luther in 1926. The Threatts were an African American family who got the land in Oklahoma's 1889 land run. The building remains, and plans are underway for it to reopen as a museum.

Round Barn. Arcadia's Round barn was built in 1898. Today it houses a nice visitor's center and museum.

Tuton Drug Store. The Tuton Drug Store opened around the corner from the Round Barn in 1917. It originally housed First State Bank of Arcadia. The bank sold the building to Thomas Tuton, whose family operated the drug store until 1941. Today it is an antique store (for sale last time I went by).

Horseshoe Bar. The Horseshoe Bar claims it has been a beer joint in Youkon since 1906. I don't know what they did during prohibition. They have many photos of Old Time Youkon.

Chisholm Trail. The Chisholm Trail went through Youkon and there are some interesting markers and museums.

Fort Reno. Fort Reno was established in 1875 to support the US Army after a Cheyenne uprising in 1874. It remained in use as a Cavalry remount station until 1949.

Mohawk Lodge. The Mohawk Lodge Indian Store in Clinton was opened in 1892. It was the first trading post in Indian Territory and it's still going strong.

New Mexico

New Mexico is old. There are hundreds of pueblos, some of which are hundreds of years old. In addition, there are churches and buildings still in use that are centuries old, and many of them were on the 1926 alignment of Route 66. I have skipped most of these places, and instead I have focused on sites of a more recent vintage that would have been noticed by Route 66 travelers.

Richardson's Store. The ruins of Richardson's Store and Sinclair Station is on Old Route 66 in Montoya. It opened in 1925 and closed in the mid-1970s when the owner died.

Sacred Heart Catholic Church. The Sacred Heart Catholic Church in Dillia was built in 1900 on what became the 1926 alignment of Route 66.

Senora de la Luz Church. The Senora de la Luz Church was built in Canoncito in the 1880s. It has a haunting look, especially because of the hillside cemetery with wooden crosses as grave markers. Ansel Adams photographed this church, and it remains a popular scene for local artists.

Santa Fe. Santa Fe was founded in 1610 as a Spanish colony, but here was a settlement there beginning in about 900. Today, Santa Fe is a bustling art community and tourist destination with a population of about 80,000; *however*, in 1926, Santa Fe had only 6,000 residents. The Palace of the Governors, bunches of old churches and hundreds of buildings lined the road for hundreds years before Route 66 was established.

La Bajada Hill. La Bajada Hill was on the primary road leading into Santa Fe in 1926. It was part of the El Camino Real de Tierra Adentro trade route between Mexico City and Santa Fe, which was established in about 1598. When it was incorporated into the original alignment of Route 66, it was so steep that cars with gravity fed fuel lines would have to drive up the hill backwards for the fuel to reach the engine. It was abandoned in 1932 when Route 66 was realigned to flow south of Santa Fe, but it can still be traversed in an appropriately rigged four-wheel-drive vehicle or by hiking.

La Fonda Hotel. Beginning in the 1880s, the Fred Harvey Company built a series of hotels and restaurants at railroad stations in the Southwest. These railroad stations often were on the roads that became Route 66. The Harvey House hotels and restaurants were luxurious and also were noteworthy because they were some of the only establishments that welcomed Blacks. The 1921 La Fonda Hotel on Santa Fe's Plaza was a Harvey House. It is on a site that has had an inn continuously since 1607 and is claimed to be the oldest hotel corner in America.

Red Ball Café. The Red Ball Café on the outskirts of downtown Albuquerque began serving the Wimpy Burger in 1922. It was closed the last time I went by, but I'm holding out hope that it will be serving Wimpy burgers again soon.

Rex Hotel. Gallup's Rex Hotel was on the original Route 66 and today houses the Rex Museum, which covers the history of Gallup and has many historical photographs of street scenes along Route 66.

Arizona

Petrified Forrest and Painted Desert. Arizona's Route 66 passed through the Petrified Forrest and the Painted Desert. Travelers could stay at the Painted Desert Inn, which opened in the early 20th Century. It now is a museum with displays highlighting the building's history, Route 66 and the Civilian Conservation Corps.

Weatherford Hotel. The Weatherford Hotel in Flagstaff opened in 1900. It was supposed to have been a favorite stop for Wyatt Earp. It's still there featuring 11 guest rooms and two terrific restaurants and bars.

Orpheum Theater. The Orpheum Theater opened in Flagstaff in 1917. It was closed for years but was renovated and reopened in 2002. It has movies and live entertainment.

Lowell Observatory. The Lowell Observatory in Flagstaff was established in 1894. This is where Pluto was discovered in 1930. It has a 24 inch Clark Refracting telescope that was built in 1926 for $20,000.

Frey Marcus Hotel. Williams Arizona is my favorite Route 66 town. The 1908 Frey Marcos was the Harvey House Hotel. It is located in the Williams Depot. It no longer serves guests, but part of the original structure houses the Grand Canyon Railway Gift Shop.

Grand Canyon Hotel. The Grand Canyon Hotel in Williams was opened in 1891 and is the oldest hotel in Arizona. After I-40 bypassed Williams, the Grand Canyon Hotel was closed and sat empty for 35 years. It recently was reopened. It's a bit rustic, but it's right on the main drag of Route 66 and provides an interesting glimpse into the past.

Sultana Bar. The Sultana Bar in Williams opened in 1906 and is the oldest bar in Arizona. There is an original tin ceiling that must be 15 feet high. There are trophies, including a moose a mountain lion, a caribou and an elk. This place looks like it hasn't changed a bit since the day it opened.

Red Garter B&B. The Red Garter Bed and Bakery in Williams is in a restored 1897 saloon and brothel. It remained a house of ill repute well into the 20th century and it probably was a pretty dicey place when Route 66 opened in 1926. Today, the cribs are rented out as nicely appointed guest rooms.

Beale Hotel. Actor Andy Devine's father bought the Beale Hotel in 1906, and Andy Devine grew up there. In 1923, the rates ranged from a $1.50 to $4.00 per night. The Devine's sold the Beale in 1926 just as Route 66 was opening. It has been closed for years.

Cool Springs Store. The Cool Springs Store opened outside of Kingman on the Oatman Highway in the early 1920s. It was an important stopping point for gas and supplies along Route 66. In the 1930s there were eight cabins and a restaurant. Today all that's left is a small store and rock gift shop.

Oatman Hotel. In 1926, Oatman still was an active mining town. The Oatman Hotel, which opened in 1902, is where Clark Gable and Carol Lombard eloped. Guestrooms no longer are available but there is a cool bar and restaurant.

California

Old Trails Bridge. Route 66 travelers in 1926 crossed the Colorado River into California over the Old Trails Bridge, which was completed in 1916. This bridge was featured in the movies *The Grapes of Wrath* and *Easy Rider*. It was bypassed when I-40 was built and then was converted into a pipeline bridge.

El Garces Hotel. The EL Garces Hotel in Needles was the crown jewel of the Harvey House Hotels. It was built in 1908 and was a Route 66 staple until it closed in 1949. It has been partially renovated and since 2014 has served as the El Garces Intermodal Transportation Facility, which so far as I can tell is a fancy way for saying it's an unmanned Amtrak station.

Roy's. Amboy's famous Roy's was not opened as a garage until 1927, but the nearby Amboy crater was formed about 6,000 years ago. It last erupted about 500 years ago. It is 250 feet high in 1,500 feet across. Climbing is allowed and there is a walking trail to the top that will let you peer into the crater.

Casa del Desierto. Today Main Street in Barstow follows Business 15, but in 1926, it followed the railroad tracks about a quarter of a mile away. The Casa del Desierto, which was built in 1911, was Barstow's Harvey House Hotel. It now serves as the Amtrak depot. The Barstow Route 66 Mother Road Museum and the Western America Railroad Museum also are there.

Iron Hog Saloon. The Iron Hog Saloon in Oro Grande opened as a Wells Fargo switching station in the 1890s. It has been a bar since the 1930s. Roy Rogers' ranch is nearby. Roy and Dale Evans were frequent guests, and their initials are carved into the bar. It has been featured in the movies *Easy Rider*, *Poker Run* and *Erin Brockovich*.

Sycamore Inn. The Sycamore Inn in Rancho Cucamonga started as a stagecoach stop in 1848. It has been operating since then and ever nicer structures, and now is an upscale restaurant.

Wolfe's Market. Wolfe's Market has been operating on Route 66 in Claremont since 1917. It has been in its current location since 1935. It's still a great place to have a sandwich while passing through this portion of Route 66.

Aztec Hotel. The Aztec Hotel opened in Monrovia in 1924. It's supposed to be one of the best examples of Mayan revival architecture. So, you think they would've called at the Mayan Hotel. The Aztec was closed for years. The restaurant and bar were reopened for a while, but they again are closed.

Rose Bowl. The Rose Bowl is not right on Route 66, but it opened in Pasadena in 1922. Surely, many Route 66 travelers of the day made short detour to view this wonderful stadium.

Rite Spot Restaurant. The Rite Spot Restaurant in Pasadena claims to have invented the cheeseburger in 1924. Louie's Lunch in New Haven Connecticut may have an argument there. Louie's, a Yalie hang out for over a century, claims to have invented the hamburger in 1900.

Lowe's State Theater. The original terminus of Route 66 was at the intersection of Broadway and 7th Street in Los Angeles. In 1926 it was the busiest intersection the United States with over 500,000 people crossing the streets each day. Lowe's State Theater, which opened on this intersection in 1921, is the most profitable theater location in Southern California entertainment history.

This is one of my favorites. The Negro Motorist Green Book was published in the mid-20th century to give black travelers a guide to traveling the country to places where they would be welcome, and more importantly, safe. I never had heard of The Green Book until one of my blog followers sent me a link to an article about it. Since then, The Green Book has become better known following the release of the acclaimed movie Green Book *in 2018. This story predates the release of the movie.*

The Negro Motorist Green Book

A FEW DAYS AGO MY FRIEND Phil Devlin from my hometown of Haddam, Connecticut, sent me a link to an article about The National Park Service Route 66 Corridor Preservation Program's Route 66 *Green Book* Project. The Project focuses on *The Negro Motorist Green Book*, which was published by Victor Green between 1936 and 1966 to give black travelers a guide to the towns, hotels, restaurants and other businesses that would welcome them. The Project's purpose is to identify the properties along Route 66 listed in *The Green Book* and preserve those that still exist.

During the Jim Crow era, racial discrimination was not limited to the Deep South. Blacks traveling across country had to deal not only with segregation and businesses that would not serve them. They also had to contend with so called "Sundown Towns," that posted signs requiring blacks to leave town all together after sundown. Over half of all of the counties along Route 66 had Sundown Towns.

This presented problems for black travelers greater than just not being welcome. Blacks had to time their trips so as not to pass through a Sundown Town after dark. If a black traveler needed gasoline or assistance due to a breakdown, he or she not only could not count on help from a Sundown Town, they might be subject to harassment, arrest or worse. Even in towns where black friendly establishments were available, they often were clustered in predominantly black neighborhoods that were miles off the main route. These circumstances made travel by blacks not only inconvenient, but outright dangerous. Victor Green set out to help blacks avoid these issues during their travels.

Victor Green was born in New York City in 1892. In the 1930s, Green began compiling data about stores in the New York area that would accept blacks and in 1936 he published a guide to those stores. He based his guide on similar publications that had been used by Jews who experienced their own forms of discrimination.

The book was popular, and Green expanded it to include hotels, restaurants, gas stations, bars, barber shops, and other businesses in the New York area and eventually throughout the United States. He opened his own publishing house where he produced and distributed 15,000 copies of his book annually. In 1947, he started his own Vacation Reservation Service, which was a travel agency to help blacks better plan their trips. By 1949 his guides had expanded to include Bermuda and Mexico.

Green was an optimist. In the introduction to his first book he said, "There will be a day sometime in the near future when this guide will not have to be published. That is when we as a race will have equal rights and privileges in the United States."

That came to pass, but not in his lifetime. Green died in 1960 and his wife Alma kept putting out *The Green Book* until 1966. Adoption of the Civil Rights Act of 1964, which made most forms of racial discrimination illegal, fostered an air of optimism and hope among many in the black community. That optimism persuaded Alma to discontinue publication of the book based on the somewhat naive belief that the laws would be embraced throughout the country, thus rendering *The Green Book* unnecessary.

Candacy Taylor is the head of the Route 66 *Green Book* Project. She is an author, photographer and cultural critic who has traveled over 300,000 miles throughout the United States documenting stories about American culture. She accidentally came across *The Green Book* while she was conducting research for her recently published book *Moon Route 66 Road Trip*. *The Green Book* made her think of Route 66 in a new light through the realization that not all Americans had a shared romanticism of the Mother Road.

Candacy is conducting The *Green Book* Project in conjunction with the National Park Service. A Park Service release on the internet includes a link to a 15-page spreadsheet purporting to include of all the Route 66 businesses that were listed in *The Green Book*. The list actually is a composite of black friendly businesses taken from *The Green Book* and several other black oriented travel guides. The list is incomplete on its face because Chicago is not mentioned. Additionally, it lists only lodging and eating establishments, and omits gas stations, barber shops and other businesses that were in *The Green Book* and other black travel guidebooks. Despite these shortcomings, I looked to see what I might find. The results were more than a little interesting.

The overwhelming majority of lodging and eating establishments were boardinghouses run by black married women. Los Angeles has many remaining *Green Book* sites, but other than in Los Angeles, almost all of the rest of these sites have been demolished. Of the buildings that remain, a substantial number are YMCAs, are located in train stations or were Harvey House Hotels. Those hotels and related restaurants, all of which welcomed blacks, were built and operated by the Fred Harvey Company along railroad lines in the West between 1875 and the mid-20th century.

Of the 15 pages of listings, about 11.5 pages are from Springfield, Illinois, St. Louis, Tulsa, Oklahoma City and Los Angeles, with Los Angeles accounting for five full pages. That leaves only 3.5 pages for all of the remaining Route 66 towns. The concentration of black friendly businesses in cities is unsurprising because blacks tended to stay in cities to avoid the hostility that likely would have greeted them in a substantial portion of rural America.

There are only two hotels listed in which I have stayed, and both are featured in my soon to be published book *Route 66 Top 10s*. They are the La Posada in Winslow (a Harvey House Hotel) and the El Rey in Santa Fe.

The only other hotels of which I am familiar are the Cactus Motel (now an RV park) in Tucumcari, NM; the DeAnza Motor Hotel in

Albuquerque, NM (closed); the El Rancho Motel in Holbrook, AZ; the Du Beau Hotel in Flagstaff, AZ; the Fray Marcos Hotel in Williams, AZ (closed Harvey House); the El Garces Hotel in Needles, CA (closed Harvey House); and the Casa del Desierto Hotel in Barstow, CA (closed Harvey House).

I have never heard of a single one of the restaurants.

So, if *The Green Book* is to be believed, other than the Harvey House chain there does not appear to be a single "classic" Route 66 hotel or restaurant that would accept blacks; *however*, that is not necessarily the case. Perusing copies of *The Green Book* available online gives the feel that *The Green Book* was intended to be a useful, but not exhaustive, list of businesses that would welcome blacks. Nonetheless, the complete absence of the classic spots is striking. It's no wonder *The Green Book* was considered The Bible of Black Travel.

Candacy Taylor's *Moon Route 66 Road Trip* lists four places as among the best of the remaining Route 66 *Green Book* properties. They are the DuBeau Hotel in Flagstaff (now a hostel); the DeAnza Motor Lodge in Albuquerque (closed but with renovation plans); Clifton's in Los Angeles (going strong since 1935); and the Warren Hotel in Tulsa.

Of these, Clifton's shines not only as a surviving *Green Book* site, but as a Route 66 icon. Clifton's is a five story cafeteria style restaurant that opened in 1935 at Broadway and 7th St. in Los Angeles, which was the original terminus of the 1926 alignment of Route 66. Owner Clifford Clifton would not turn away anyone who was hungry. Rather than charging a fixed price, customers would pay what they could afford. Clifton's closed in 2011, but new owners have given it a $10 million facelift and it has re-opened in all its original splendor.

The story of Tulsa's Warren Hotel is not so uplifting.

Tulsa's Greenwood District was said to be the wealthiest black community in the United States. On May 31 and June 1, 1921, a group of whites instigated the Tulsa Race Riot when they attacked the area and burned it to the ground. Between 40 and 300 people were killed and over 800 more were injured. The black community rebounded and rebuilt, including the construction of the Warren Hotel. The building still is standing but the hotel is not in operation.

I have a book coming out in the next week or so called *Route 66 Top 10s*. It lists my top 10 favorite Route 66 rides, towns, towns with Pop Art signs, roadside attractions, hotels, bars, restaurants and drive-ins, with honorable mentions in each category. Tulsa comes in as my No. 4 Route 66 town and is represented in all of the other categories of Top 10s. Despite all this knowledge of Tulsa, I had never heard of the Tulsa Race Riot or the Warren Hotel before writing this blog. But I'll bet all blacks who traveled Route 66 during the years *The Green Book* was published knew all about the Riot and the Hotel. And today's generation of blacks gets its stories about Route 66 from folks who were shunned rather than welcomed on the Mother Road.

Upon reflection, I cannot recall any advertising directed toward or featuring blacks in any of the thousands of Route 66 artifacts I have seen. In fact, I rarely see any blacks touring Route 66. I certainly see many more European whites than American blacks. Given that over half of the counties across Route 66 had Sundown Towns, it is not surprising that blacks do not share the fond nostalgic feelings about Route 66 that white America embraces.

All this makes the Route 66 *Green Book* Project all the more interesting and important. Identifying and preserving the businesses that were in *The Green Book* is only part of the Project. There also will be a book, a traveling exhibition, a digital interactive map, a board game and a virtual reality platform. These multi-media formats will make a story that should have been told long ago accessible to everyone from scholars to casual Route 66 travelers.

I'm already excited about it. While writing this article I have come across some *Green Book* businesses that still are thriving but to which I never have been, as well as a dozen or so that are listed as still standing, but for which I can find no reference through internet searches. I can't wait to go find them.

Endnote: *Candacy finished the project, which launched its three year tour in June 2020 as a Smithsonian Institution Traveling Exhibition. She also published her book* Overground Railroad: The Green Book *and the Roots of Black Travel in America in January 2020.*

Bonnie and Clyde were from Dallas, but they spent lots of time on Route 66. This story tells about their most notable Route 66 travels and crimes. Many of the sites still exist and you can visit them when you explore Route 66.

Bonnie and Clyde on Route 66

Bonnie and Clyde were a team of Depression era bandits who robbed gas stations, grocery stores and an occasional bank. They were friends with Pretty Boy Floyd and Baby Face Nelson, and contemporaries of John Dillinger. They were glamorized in the 1967 movie *Bonnie and Clyde*. But they were not so glamorous in life.

Bonnie Parker was born in 1910 in a Rowena, Texas, a small-town Southwest of Dallas. In 1925, during her second year in High School, she met Roy Thornton, dropped out of school and married him a week before her 16th birthday. They had a troubled marriage and split in 1929, never seeing each other again; *however,* they never divorced, and she was wearing her wedding ring when she died.

Clyde Barrow was born in 1909 in Tellico, Texas, a small town Southeast of Dallas. His first arrest was in 1926 for failing to return a rented car. A series of arrests followed, and he wound up in the Easton Prison farm in 1930. He led a violent life at Easton but was paroled in 1932. He quickly returned to crime, focusing on small robberies. His weapon of choice was the Browning Automatic Rifle.

Bonnie met Clyde in 1930 at the home of a mutual friend. They were attracted to each other immediately. Soon after they met Clyde went to prison for burglary. He escaped using a gun Bonnie smuggled to him. He soon was captured and returned to prison.

Nineteen thirty-two was a big year for the Barrow gang.

In April, Bonnie participated in a hardware store robbery for which she was jailed, but the grand jury did not indict her and she was released in June.

While Bonnie was in jail, Clyde robbed a store in Hillsboro, Texas, and the store owner was killed.

In August, while Bonnie was visiting her mother, Clyde and other gang members were involved in a police altercation in Stringtown, Oklahoma, in which a deputy was killed, and the sheriff was severely wounded.

In October the gang killed a store owner in a robbery in Sherman, Texas.

On Christmas day, W. D. Jones was initiated into the gang when he and Clyde killed a man in Temple, Texas while stealing his car.

A couple of weeks later, on January 6, 1933, Bonnie, Clyde and Jones killed a Terrant County deputy when they accidentally wandered into a trap set for some other criminals.

Bonnie and Clyde operated all over the mid-west, so it's no surprise that they would wind up on Route 66.

In late 1932, Bonnie and Clyde were hiding out at a motor court in Carthage, Missouri. Carthage residents claim the hide out was at White's Court Motel, which was opened on Route 66 in 1927 as a motel, gas station and café. They pulled off a series of robberies in the Carthage area. On the 29th of November, they robbed the Farmers and Miners Bank in Oronogo, Missouri, and fled in two getaway cars after a gunfight.

White's Court Motel now is called the Red Rock Apartments. To get there, leave Downtown Carthage on Route 66 (Mo. Highway 96). Take a right at the Kel-Lake Motel onto Old Route 66. The Red Rock Apartments are on the left a few hundred yards down Old Route 66. They are being renovated and the name "Red Rock Apartments" might change, but you won't have trouble finding the place.

In January 1933, in Springfield, Missouri, some wrestling matches were being held in the Shriner's Mosque on Route 66 at 601 E. St. Louis St. Motorcycle policeman Tom Purcell spotted a car with two men and a woman who appeared to be scoping out cars. Purcell pulled the car over, but when he approached, Clyde or W. D. Jones stepped out of the car with a shotgun and told Purcell to get in. Bonnie and Clyde sometimes would kidnap a local resident to guide them out of town after a robbery. That's why they purloined Purcell. They sped through several towns, including Webb City and Joplin, looking unsuccessfully for a car to steal. They wound up in Oronogo, Missouri, where they forced Purcell to steal a battery for them, then they released Purcell unharmed.

When recounting the incident to a local newspaper, Purcell said that during the ride, Bonnie chain smoked cigarettes and she, Clyde and W. D. constantly used profane language. Purcell claimed that upon his release he asked for a return of his handgun; Clyde told him not to push his luck.

In March 1933, Buck Barrow was pardoned for crimes for which he was in prison. He and his wife Blanche quickly joined Bonnie, Clyde and the rest of the gang where they were hiding out in an apartment over a garage at 3347½ Oak Ridge Drive (at 34th Street), less than a mile off Route 66, in Joplin, Missouri.

Local residents informed the police about suspicious activity at the address. They never opened the blinds, no neighbors ever visited, and they never ventured out into the neighborhood. There was raucous noise late into the night. On April 13, a five-man squad armed with handguns went to the apartment expecting to confront some bootleggers.

A gunfight ensued. Clyde and perhaps others were armed with Browning Automatic Rifles, and two of the policemen were killed. Bonnie laid down covering fire as the gang went into the garage for their car for a get-away. Clyde burst the car through the closed garage doors. Bonnie and Blanche ran to the street and jumped into the car at the last minute. Bonnie, Clyde, Buck and W. D. Jones all were wounded.

The gang escaped, but they left all their possessions, including Buck and Blanche's wedding license, Buck's parole papers (only three weeks old), a bunch of weapons, a poem Bonnie had written called "Suicide Sal" and a camera with several rolls of film. The Joplin Globe newspaper developed the film, which had the now famous photos of Bonnie and Clyde brandishing weapons and the photo of Bonnie posing in front of a car smoking a cigar and holding a pistol.

This incident and the publication of the photos in newspapers throughout the country brought Bonnie and Clyde to national attention. In the following months, they committed robberies from Minnesota to Louisiana. Their notoriety made travel and lodging more difficult, and they often had to camp to avoid notice by the police.

The Joplin apartment can be rented through Airbnb for about $100 per night. It has limited reviews, but they are good.

In July 1933, they were discovered at the Red Crown Tourist Court in Platte City, Missouri. A large contingent of police armed with automatic weapons raided the hideout. Though far outnumbered, the gang made a daring escape. Buck received a severe headwound. Five days later the gang was surrounded at a camp near Dexter, Iowa. In the ensuing gunfight, Bonnie, Clyde and W. D. Jones escaped on foot, but Buck was shot in the back and Blanche was captured. Buck died five days later.

Things were not going well for Bonnie and Clyde. They were on the run and hiding was increasingly difficult. They had been hold-up in Northeastern Oklahoma and committed a series of petty robberies along the Route 66 towns or Pryor, Afton and Miami. On April 6th, 1934, in Commerce, Oklahoma, Constable Cal Campbell and Police Chief Percy Boyd went to the corner of E 60 Rd. and Tahoe Ave. to investigate a suspicious car that was parked there. They thought they were going to confront a car full of drunks. As they approached the car, it attempted to speed away, but slid in the mud and went into a ditch.

Instead of finding some drunks, Clyde and gang member Henry Methvin emerged firing automatic weapons. Campbell was killed and Boyd was wounded in the head and kidnapped. Barrow flagged down a car at gunpoint to help dislodge his car from the mud. By this time numerous townspeople had gathered at the scene, but none interfered.

Boyd later claimed that the Barrows treated him nicely, and that Bonnie helped dress his wounds. He eventually was released in Fort Scott, Kansas. He was given a clean shirt, a few dollars and instructions to tell the world that Bonnie did not smoke cigars.

Cal Campbell was the last person known to have been killed by the Barrow gang.

Commerce resident Doyle Alsbury saw the shooting and was one of the local gawkers. In 2013 when I was writing the first edition of *The Route 66 Motorcycle Party Guide*, I called the Commerce Chamber of

Commerce to find some details of this incident. It turned out Mr. Alsbury still was alive and had moved to Oklahoma City. I tried to contact him, but I was unsuccessful. That sure would have been an interesting conversation.

There is a monument to Cal Campbell in front of City Hall on Mickey Mantle Blvd. in Commerce, but that's not the site of the shooting and kidnapping. To find that site, head out of Commerce on Main St. toward Miami. Go right at E 60 Rd. to the next intersection, which is Tahoe Ave (there is no street sign).

A little over a month after Cal Campbell's murder, on May 23, 1934, Bonnie and Clyde were killed in an ambush while driving in Bienville Parish, Louisiana. They were traveling alone to visit Henry Methvin's family, and Methvin's father ratted them out for a reward. Over 130 rounds pierced the car, and the bodies were so bullet ridden that embalming was difficult. Bonnie was 24 and Clyde was 25 years old.

It had been a bad year for gangsters. John Dillinger, Pretty Boy Floyd, Baby Face Nelson, and Bonnie and Clyde all were killed.

Clyde is buried in the Barrow family plot next to his brother Buck in the Western Heights Cemetery in Dallas.

Bonnie is buried in northwest Dallas at Crown Hill Memorial Park.

Blanche was sentenced to 10 years in the Missouri State Penitentiary for assault with the intent to commit murder. She served six years. In 1940, she married Eddie Frasure. Eddie died in 1969 and Blanche died of cancer in 1988 at age 77. Her memoir, *My Life with Bonnie and Clyde*, was published posthumously. She is buried in the Grant Hill Memorial Park in Dallas.

W. D. Jones had left the Barrow gang and moved to Houston, where he worked on farms. He was arrested and was in jail when Bonnie and Clyde were killed. He was convicted of murder without malice and received a 15-year sentence in Huntsville Prison in Texas. He was killed in Houston in August 1974 when trying to gain entrance to a friend's home at 3:55 in the morning. He is buried in Brookside Memorial Park.

Henry Methvin was the last surviving member of the Barrow gang. He was convicted of the murder of Cal Campbell and sentenced to death. His sentence was commuted to life in prison, and he was paroled in 1942. He was killed in 1848 by a train while crossing some tracks when he was drunk. He is buried in Sulphur, Louisiana.

Bonnie and Clyde had a mystique during their lifetimes that remains today. But there was nothing romantic about them. They were petty thieves who killed at least 13 people, including nine policemen. Often, they killed for the sake of killing. Still, its alluring to visit the sites of their misdeeds.

From the beginning of its 50 year run, the Coral Court was both a high end destination that attracted families and also served as a low rent rendezvous venue. It also had a role in one of the country's most infamous and gruesome kidnappings

The Coral Court Caper (Part 1)

The Coral Court Motel was opened by John Carr as an upscale motor court in 1942 in the then largely undeveloped St. Louis suburb of Marlborough to take advantage of the large US population movement that began during WWII. It was on Route 66 at 7755 Watson Road, and originally consisted of an office building and 10 separate single-story bungalows, each with two rooms separated by a two-car indoor garage. Construction costs reportedly were $7,000, but that sounds cheap even in 1942 dollars. It was intended to be the finest motel in the St. Louis area, and a natural stopping point for travelers heading west from Chicago on Route 66, which still was the best highway to the west.

The original 10 buildings were referred to as the "Traditional Units." They were made of golden glazed bricks and opaque glass blocks resulting in a slick streamlined art deco look. In 1946, 23 additional two room buildings were added. These were referred to as the "Mae West Units" because the front bays were curved, and so was Mae West. In 1953, three two story buildings, each with eight rooms, were added, and a pool was added in the early 1960s. The pool was popular with guests, and neighborhood children were allowed the run of it.

When the Coral Court opened in 1942, Route 66 had been a National Highway for 16 years. Marlboro had not been developed significantly; *however*, the Duplex Tourist Cottages (now the Duplex Motel) and the Chippewa Tourist Cottages (now the Chippewa Motel) had been operating nearby since 1937. By the 1950s, there were at least 13 additional Motels in Marlboro, including the Wayside Motel, which was across the street from the Coral Court and still operates. But the Coral Court's distinctive architecture made it stand out from its competitors. It gained a national reputation, and loyal families would make annual visits.

The Coral Court was a "no tell-motel" situation from the beginning. Even in 1942, both nightly and hourly rates were available, and the privacy of the enclosed parking spaces made the Coral Court popular with both adults and hormone raging teens seeking a low rent rendezvous.

Rumors about owner John Carr's past added to the Coral Court's nefarious reputation. Although Carr universally was viewed as a generous man who took pride in the meticulous upkeep of his motel, there were rumors that he had been a financial guy for the mob and that he owned brothels in Downtown St. Louis. He held card games in the basement of the office building, which was cooled naturally by an underground stream. Also, there supposedly was a secret underground passageway from that basement to a house across the street to be used if a quick get-away was needed.

It was an odd mixture of respectability and seediness. Although it always was known for clandestine trysts, it was so nice that it attracted families and even newlyweds.

Shellee Graham published a book called *Tales from the Coral Court*, which has dozens of reminiscences of former employees, motel guests and others who had associations with the Coral Court. Route 66 author Michael Wallis is quoted saying:

> "Just after the motor court opened in 1941, young men going off to war stayed there with their wives and sweethearts. Some of those GIs never returned. There are women whose hair has grown gray that recall every detail of that last night spent with their young men – wrapped in each other's arms with only the sound of passing traffic on the Mother Road to serenade them. To all those people and for so many, many more, the Coral Court was a special place – an extra special place."

On the other hand, a former housekeeper was asked "Why do you think people went to the Coral Court." She replied:

> "Well, to get that groove on, that's all I can tell you. Get that groove on. You know, they had those artificial things – you'd always find those tricky things, play toys. You'd always find them in the room – all sizes, all shapes. That was one of the funnier things."

I-44 bypassed Route 66 in Marlboro in 1972. Unlike many businesses, the Coral Court remained prosperous, at least for a while, largely due to John's keeping the property pristine and the Motel's privacy.

John Carr died in 1984, the same year Route 66 was decommissioned. John's wife Jessie did not run the motel herself and she allowed it to go into disrepair.

My Ole Miss fraternity brother ("Rah, Rah Rega. Alpha Tau Omega…") Steve King is a life-long St. Louis resident who recalls the evolution of the Coral Court from the 1970s through the 1990s. He told me that the Coral Court always had a dicey reputation, but that during the 1970s and into the 1980s, the place was well kept. However, by the end of the '80s, things had deteriorated. He says:

> "Coral Courts, otherwise known as the no tell motel, had a well-deserved reputation as a place where one could 'discretely' screw around. The rooms had garages, so your car was safe from prying eyes. The art deco was cool, but the rooms were not all that neat. Bad mattresses, bad plumbing and you were lucky if more than one light worked.
>
> Later in the night on some weekends there was literally a traffic jam around the place. Starting at around 10:00 or 11:00 there would be a line in the office to get a room.
>
> I was there a couple of times and had had a few, so I don't remember all the details."

Jessie claimed she was disinclined to sell the Motel unless the buyer would agree to restore it to its historical grandeur. There were no takers.

She tried to sell the property to developers, but multiple deals fell through. In the early 1990s, some of the buildings were condemned and the Motel closed. In the meantime, local residents established the Coral Court Preservation Society and got the Motel listed on the National Register of Historic Places. But insufficient funds were raised to preserve the property and the Motel was closed in 1993. It was demolished in 1995 for the construction of a housing development. Unbelievably, on the first day of demolition, the original sign was torn down and intentionally destroyed.

Today, the Coral Court's site has a subdivision of single family homes. The only remnants are the original stone gates and pillars. Efforts are underway to place a historic marker on the site. You'd think that would be easy to accomplish, but apparently, it's not. It turns out the developers of the site do not want the tourist traffic that a historical marker might attract.

During demolition, preservationists were permitted to dismantle one of the two room units for future reconstruction and display at the National Museum of Transportation, at 2933 Barrett Station Road, Kirkwood, Missouri 63122. A few original furnishings also were saved. Unfortunately, many of the tiles, bricks and other portions of the building were damaged or destroyed during dismantling and transportation, and not enough could be preserved to reconstruct an entire unit. However, the Museum used the best of the salvaged materials to build a display of the original façade of the building with a replica Coral Court sign and a vintage Corvette in the driveway.

While the Coral Court had a half century run of squeaky-springed fun as one of the best-known Route 66 motor courts, it also was part of one of the most horrific kidnappings of the 20th Century. Stay tuned for next week's posting of The Coral Court Caper (Part 2).

This is the story of the kidnapping of Bobby Greenlease, the part the Coral Court played in the affair and the fate of the kidnappers.

The Coral Court Caper (Part 2)

Last week's post followed the rise and demise of the Coral Court Motel, which opened in 1942, and was the most notorious no tell motel along Route 66 for half a century. It was a stylish place with an enclosed garage for each room that offered privacy for carnal capers at hourly rates.

But in 1953, the privacy provided shelter for more sinister purposes.

Carl Hall had attended the Kemper Military School in the 1930s with Paul Greenlease, the adopted son of millionaire General Motors car dealer Robert Greenlease. Hall despised Paul and planned to do his family ill for years. In 1953, Hall was living with Bonnie Heady in St. Joseph, Missouri. They both were drug addicted alcoholics who acted on Hall's hatred for Paul Greenlease by committing one of the most notorious kidnappings in U.S. history.

On September 28, 1953, Heady showed up at the Notre Dame de Scion Catholic School in Kansas City, Missouri, and convinced Sister Morand to believe that she was the aunt of Robert Greenlease's six-year old son Bobby, that Bobby's mother had suffered a heart attack, and had asked her to pick Bobby up from the school. Sister Morand consented. Heady took Bobby by the hand and led him to a Toadman Cab Company taxi driven by Willard Creech. Bobby went along without protest.

The taxi dropped Heady and Bobby at the Katz Drug Store on Main St. in Kansas City. Hall picked them up in a 1952 Ford Sedan with Kansas license plates. They took Bobby to Overland Park just outside of Kansas City.

In a series of ransom calls, Hall assured Mr. Greenlease that his son was being treated well and would be returned safely upon the payment of $600,000. Mr. Greenlease was 71 years old. He adored his only naturally born son Bobby and was willing to meet any demand to save him. He ignored the advice or assistance of the local police and the FBI, and October 5, 1953, paid the ransom, which was delivered in a duffle bag filled with $10 and $20-dollar bills thrown out of a moving Cadillac along Highway 40 East of Kansas City.

Hall and Heady drove to St. Louis and rented a room at 4505 Arsenal St. They went on a bender. They fought. Eventually Heady passed out, and Hall called a prostitute named Sandra O'Day, picked her up in a cab driven by John Hagar, and checked into the Coral Court. Hagar became suspicious because Hall was flaunting lots of money. He reported this to Joe Costello, his mobster boss. Costello contacted Lt. Louis Shoulders, a crooked cop who was on Costello's payroll, who arrested Hall on October 6, 1953.

Costello and Shoulders figured that Hall was an embezzler and tried to shake him down. Instead, he confessed to the kidnapping and ratted Heady out. The police arrested Heady at the Arsenal St. room.

The Bobby Greenlease kidnapping garnered the most national press coverage of any kidnapping since the abduction of Charles Lindberg, Jr. in 1932. The $600,000 ransom that Hall and Heady demanded was the largest in U.S. history; the ransom for the Lindberg Baby was only $50,000. Richard Bruno Hauptman was convicted of kidnapping Baby Lindberg in 1934 and was executed in the electric chair in 1936, four years after the kidnapping.

Justice was quicker for the kidnappers of Bobby Greenlease.

On October 7, Hall and Heady admitted to the kidnapping and admitted that Hall had killed Bobby Greenlease with a gunshot to his head almost immediately after the abduction. Later that day, the police recovered Bobby Greanlease's body, which had been buried in Heady's St. Joseph back yard under some recently planted flowers.

On October 30, 1953, Hall and Heady pleaded guilty to kidnapping and murder before Judge Albert Reeves in federal court in Kansas City. On November 19, they were found guilty, and the jury recommended the death penalty after only an hour and eight minutes of deliberation. Fifteen minutes after the verdict was announced, Judge Reeves sentenced Hall and Heady to death.

Hall and Heady were executed together on December 18, 1953, in the gas chamber at the Missouri State Penitentiary in Jefferson City. Hall was pronounced dead at 12:12 a.m., and Heady was pronounced dead 20 seconds later. It had been 81 days from the date of the kidnapping to the date the death penalty was carried out. They had swift justice in those days!

Heady was one of only two women executed by federal authorities since the hanging Mary Suratt, who had been implicated in the planning of President Lincoln's assassination. The other woman was Esther Rosenberg, who with her husband Julius, had been executed after being convicted of giving the Russians nuclear secrets.

Only $228,000 of the ransom ever was found, and rumors floated for years that the remaining $312,000 was stashed at the Coral Court. These rumors were buttressed by suspicions that Coral Court owner John Carr was a finance guy for the mob who operated brothels in St. Louis and used the Coral Court to launder illicit cash.

Years went by with no nothing being found. The demolition of the Coral Court in 1993 was reminiscent (albeit without the national fanfare) of Geraldo Rivera's 1986 search for swag in a secret vault in Chicago's Lexington Hotel, which had been Al Capone's headquarters from 1928-1931; *however*, the results of the Coral Court demolition were as disappointing as Geraldo's Al Capone search. No money was found.

Maybe John Carr recovered the loot from Hall's Coral Court bungalow and used it for the upkeep of his motel. It seems more likely that the missing ransom money was swept up by the mobster and the crooked cop who were involved in apprehending Hall and Heady. The mystery probably never will be solved.

Andy Warhol's Rambunctious Route 66 Ride

A FEW WEEKS AGO, my friend Kevin Collins sent me a blurb about a new book by Deborah Davis called *The Ride – Andy Warhol's Plastic Fantastic Cross Country Adventure.* The book retraced a road trip Andy Warhol took across Route 66 with three friends in 1963 to attend a party that Dennis Hopper threw for Andy. It turned out that Warhol and his gay caballeros spent only three days on Route 66. But they turned out to be three important days because the Route 66 billboards, neon signs and roadside attractions they encountered had a profound influence on the Pop Artist Andy Warhol had yet to become.

In 1962, Andy Warhol was a successful commercial artist who was making $100,000 a year as an illustrator for advertisements appearing in many leading magazines. He already had begun to produce the Pop Art for which he became famous, including his Campbell's Soup cans and his Coca Cola bottle. The problem was that nobody was noticing. He believed he had a break-out moment when some of his work was displayed at a Museum of Modern Art show. But when he offered to donate one of his paintings to MoMA, they wrote him a rejection letter telling him that "It would be unfair to accept a gift that would be shown so infrequently," and asked him to pick it up.

In June of 1963, Dennis Hopper and his wife visited Andy's home to view his work. They liked Andy and wound up purchasing a painting. When the Hoppers found out that Andy had his first major solo art show scheduled for in Los Angeles in November, the Hopper's insisted that Andy visit them in Los Angeles and offered to throw him a "… genuine Hollywood party…". He decided to travel to LA by car, and it was this trip that introduced Andy Warhol and his friends to Route 66.

As part of her research, author Deborah Davis took a road trip following Warhol's route from New York to Los Angeles. Warhol had kept all of the hotel, restaurant and other receipts from his trip, and Davis used that information to find the places Andy had visited. I was looking forward to reading about Andy Warhol's images of Route 66, but Andy's and the author's images seemed to be intermingled, so it was difficult to discern what Andy Warhol saw and what she saw. Still, the influence that Route 66 had on Andy Warhol's art was apparent, and there are some interesting insights on how traveling on Route 66 in the early 1960s compares to the 21st century experience.

Andy Warhol and his three friends set out for Los Angeles on September 24, 1963. By the next night they were in St. Louis, where they picked up Route 66. The book reveals that Andy and his friends took Route 66 not only because it still was the quickest way to get from the Great Lakes to the west coast, but also because Route 66 was an attraction in its own right, and they wanted to see it.

The travelers were not impressed with Route 66 in St. Louis. They passed by the early stages of construction of the St. Louis Arch, which would not be completed for another two years. The book says that "In St. Louis… the closest thing to a roadside attraction was a mid-size white clapboard building with a long line of ice cream aficionados waiting to be served." Ted Drewes does not seem to have changed!

After leaving St. Louis, they stopped in Villa Ridge to eat at the Diamonds Restaurant, which later was called the Tri-County Restaurant. In 1963, it billed itself as the world's largest roadside restaurant. One of Andy's traveling companions described it as "… a rather grandiose rotunda…"

Andy and his friends apparently were quite a curiosity to the local clientele. While Andy's crew had a New York Avant Garde look, the Missouri girls still looked like bobby soxers and the guys looked like farmers. Although the locals were friendly enough, Andy *et al* felt uncomfortable and didn't linger long.

Andy and Co. did not have much to say about the rest of their ride through Missouri, and in Oklahoma, they skipped off of Route 66 to travel on the faster Will Rogers Turnpike from the Missouri line to Tulsa and the Turner Turnpike from Tulsa to Oklahoma City. These roads were built by the State of Oklahoma in the late 1950s and were not part of the Federal interstate highway system that soon would by-pass most towns along Route 66.

Although the group was not much impressed by Route 66 up to this point, once in Texas, things changed. They were fascinated with the Texas plains and the vistas that went on as far as they could see. They passed by the U-Drop Inn in Shamrock and saw the Regal Reptile Farm, which still was slithering in Alanreed.

Andy especially liked the billboards and neon signs. In 1963, there were as many as 20 billboards per mile along Route 66 in the west. He loved the commercialism. Where some saw "billboard trash" he saw art. It made him feel good about being an American. He said, "I didn't ever want to live anyplace where you couldn't drive down the road and see drive-ins and giant ice cream cones and walk-in hot dogs and motel signs flashing."

They stayed at the Town House Motel on Amarillo Blvd and ate at the Big Texan Steak Ranch, which at that time was on Route 66. Just like today, they would give away a free 72 oz. steak to anybody who could eat it in an hour.

The next day, they passed Jesse's Café in Adrian, which today is the Mid-Point Café. They also went through Glenrio, which today is a ghost town, but in 1963 was "A lively little place that offered tourists a store, a gas station, a hotel and a bar."

Traveling on Route 66 in the west was proving to be precarious. I-40 had not been built, so they were traveling on the original roadway. They described the road as narrow with potholes that could cause cars to lose control. Locals said that there were "… six inches and a cigarette paper between you and death on 66…" Travelers were cautioned to carry extra water and not to get onto any side roads. But all that was worth it because Tucumcari was just ahead.

They loved the neon signs in Tucumcari. They saw the signs for The Flying M Ranch, Tee-Pee Curios, the La Cita Restaurant and the Buckaroo Motel, all of which still are there. Just as today, the best of the signs was at the Blue Swallow Motel, which featured a blue bird flapping its wings and boasted "100% Refrigerated Air." One of Andy's friends said "It was a whole new way of looking at the United States, filled with the bright, primary colors that Warhol or Lichtenstein might have painted. Especially the signs over the motels along Route 66. As we got farther west, all the signs on the motels really were Pop Art."

Andy Warhol finally made it to Los Angeles in time for his party at the Hopper's. The party was a bigger success than Andy's art show.

The show featured 32 of Andy's Campbell's Soup cans; one for each type of soup. He also brought his 7'x5' *Gold Marilyn* and portraits of Liz Taylor and Elvis. The show got poor reviews from establishment art critics, and few pieces were purchased. He sold one Campbell Soup can to Dennis Hopper for $100. He also sold his portrait of Liz for $800. The purchaser returned it to the gallery, proclaiming that "My husband hates the painting, my children hate the painting, and my friends hate the painting."

But despite the cool reception Andy's art had received from establishment critics, others perceived that a new kind of art was emerging, and that Andy Warhol was at its center.

Moreover, Andy's travels across the country, and especially his Route 66 experiences, made him view his art in a new, more vibrant light. He was re-energized, and for the first time seemed to realize that as he prospered, his art would prosper, rather than the other way around. Upon his return to New York, he consciously transformed himself into a new Andy Warhol, an Andy Warhol who was as much a piece of Pop Art as the Pop Art he created.

When his *Gold Marilyn* was offered to MoMA later that year, they gladly accepted.

Endnote: *The art show was not successful. He sold the now famous* Silver Liz *painting of Elizabeth Taylor for $800. The buyer returned it for a* *refund a week later saying: "My husband hates the painting, my children hate the painting, my friends hate the painting."*

In 2022 it sold at Christie's for $195,000,000.

This story is about the first authentic Wild West shoot out, which occurred on a location that later became part of Route 66; and about a second Wild West gunfighter who was killed near Route 66 after it has been commissioned.

The First and Last Wild West Gunfighters

The scene is familiar. A cowboy walks out of a saloon. The double doors smack the side of the building and swing back in forth as he looks for the man he knows is waiting for him. He sees his foe immediately and they stare at each other as they walk slowly to the middle of a dusty street. Their six-guns are strapped to their sides and the holsters are tied to their legs. Sometimes they say something to each other, but more often, no words are necessary. They face each other for a few moments, each flexing their hands. Then they draw almost simultaneously. Two shots ring out. They remain staring at each other until one of them falls dead. The other re-holsters his gun. Looks at his fallen prey, then walks away.

The only problem with this scene is that it almost never happened in the wild west. Plenty of folks were shot and killed, but it more likely happened by ambush or during a robbery. Very few gunmen had the balls to face off against someone else with a deadly weapon at close range. But happened sometimes, and the first time was when Wild Bill Hickok killed Davis Tutt in Springfield, Missouri on July 21, 1865.

Dave Tutt and Wild Bill were gamblers and friends. But as often happens with guys, they became enemies because of disputes about women. Wild Bill was suspected of knocking up Tutt's sister, and Tutt was constantly hitting of Wild Bill's chick, Susanna Moore. Their friendship deteriorated, and Wild Bill refused to play in any card game that included Tutt. As retaliation, Tutt supported other card players with advice and money in an attempt to cause Wild Bill to lose money.

Their animosity came to a head at the Lyon House Hotel at 218 South Avenue, which was on Springfield's Town Square. Wild Bill was in a card game and Tutt was hanging around with a bunch of his friends. Tutt was loaning the other card players money and taunting Wild Bill, but Wild Bill was winning big, and in effect was winning Tutt's money. That pissed Tutt off.

Tutt announced to the onlookers that Wild Bill owed Tutt $40.00 from a horse trade. Wild Bill acknowledged the debt and paid Tutt on the spot. Tutt then claimed Wild Bill owed him another $35.00 from an old poker game. Hickok admitted the debt, but claimed it was only $25.00. Tutt grabbed Wild Bill's gold Waltham pocket watch off the poker table and told the crowd that he would keep the watch as collateral until Wild Bill paid the $35.00.

This chapped Wild Bill beyond words, but he was in a room full of Tutt's allies, so rather than drawing a weapon and getting into a shoot-out while outnumbered, he told Tutt to return the watch. Tutt ignored Wild Bill and left the saloon with the watch.

In an attempt to goad Wild Bill into a gunfight while being outnumbered, Tutt and his friends taunted Wild Bill for a couple of days claiming Wild Bill was a welcher. Tutt bragged that he intended to wear the watch on the Springfield Town Square. Wild Bill replied that he'd kill Tutt if he tried that.

Tutt now was in a bind. He had bragged he would wear the watch in public, but if he did, he'd have to shoot it out with Wild Bill.

The next day he wore the watch on the Town Square. At a few minutes before 6:00 pm, Hickok walked onto the south side of the Square with his navy Colt in hand. Tutt came onto the northwest corner of the Square. They reportedly were about 75 yards apart.

Wild Bill demanded his watch. Tutt did not reply. They faced each other sideways. Tutt reached for his pistol. Hickock drew his and rested it across his forearm. They shot almost simultaneously. Tutt missed, but Wild Bill's shot was true. Tutt stumbled to the porch of the courthouse then back into the street, where he fell and died.

Wild Bill was charged with murder, but the charge was reduced to manslaughter. He was acquitted after a three-day trial.

Tutt was buried in the Springfield City Cemetery, but in 1883 his grave was moved to the Maple Park Cemetery, at 300 W. Grand St. in Springfield.

All this happened in the Springfield Town Square around which the original 1926 alignment of Route 66 passes. None of the original buildings remain, but there is a marker identifying the site of the shoot-out.

Wild Bill Hickok met a violent end when he was murdered By Jack McCall on August 2, 1976, in Deadwood South Dakota. At about that time, Bill Tilghman was knocking around the west as a buffalo hunter and businessman. In 1877, he opened the Crystal Palace Saloon in Dodge City, Kansas. In 1878, he became a Deputy Sheriff under Bat Masterson. He served with Wyatt Earp and his brothers and knew Doc Holiday.

Tilghman had a troubled tenure under Masterson. He was charged with several crimes, but each time the charges were dropped. Masterson also had to sell Tilghman's house in 1879 to settle a judgment.

In 1883, Tilghman became a Deputy Marshall in Dodge City, and in 1884 he was appointed City Marshall. He held that position until he resigned in 1886 to tend to his ranch, but he remained a Deputy Sheriff.

Over the succeeding years, Tilghman was involved in several gunfights. On July 4, 1888, he killed Ed Prather in a gunfight in Farmer City, Kansas. In 1889, he was involved in the Gray County War, which was fought between the towns of Ingalls and Cimarron, each of which wanted to be the county seat. One man was killed and five were wounded.

In 1892, Tilghman was appointed a Deputy U.S. Marshall in Oklahoma. The biggest outlaw in the area was Bill Doolin and his Wild Bunch Gang. Tilghman and his associates tracked down and killed most of the gang members in a series of shoot-outs during 1895, but Doolin always escaped.

In January 1896, Tilghman single-handedly captured Bill Doolin. Tilghman tracked Doolin to a resort in Eureka Springs, Arkansas. He spotted Doolin in the lobby of a bath house and arrested him without a shot being fired. Doolin was put into the Guthrie Jail but escaped before his trial. Because of the escape, Oklahoma refused to pay Tilghman the reward he had earned. Doolin later was killed by Heck Thomas in August 1896.

Although capturing Bill Doolin was the apex of Tilghman's career, he remained in law enforcement for the rest of his life.

In 1915, Tilghman produced a movie about his life called *The Passing of the Oklahoma Outlaws*. He starred in it himself. The premier was held in Chandler, Oklahoma on May 25, 1915. He toured the country showing the movie and appearing on stage to answer questions about his career. The movie originally was 96 minutes long, but only 13 minutes have survived.

In 1924 Tilghman was serving as a "special investigator." He was in Cromwell, Oklahoma, where he previously had clashed with a corrupt U.S. prohibition agent named Wiley Lynn. Tilghman confronted an intoxicated Lynn who had been shooting his gun in town. Tilghman disarmed Lynn, but Lynn pulled a second gun. He shot Tilghman several times and Tilghman died of his wounds.

Lynn was found innocent of murdering Tilghman based on self-defense. Lynn was killed in a gunfight in 1932.

Tilghman is buried in the Route 66 town of Chandler, Oklahoma.

Several of the Wild West's law officers survived Tilghman. His friend Bat Masterson died at his desk of a heart attack at the New York Telegraph in 1921. Wyatt Earp died in Los Angeles of chronic cystitis in 1929. But Tilghman was the last of the gunmen to die in a gunfight.

This story is about the funeral of Civil War General William Tecumseh Sherman, who is buried in a cemetery adjacent to the 1926 alignment of Route 66.

Sherman's Last March

CIVIL WAR GENERAL William Tecumseh Sherman was most known for his famous March to the Sea. Sherman the led 62,000 men 285 miles from Atlanta to Savanah, Georgia in only 40 days. It was described as the greatest military achievement since Julius Caesar. But Sherman was not always as self-confident as he was during his March to the Sea, nor was he always so successful as a general.

Just before the beginning of the Civil War, Sherman was Superintendent of the Louisiana State Seminary of Learning & Military Academy, which later became LSU. He was a West Point Graduate who had served in a non-combat role in the Mexican War, during which many of his contemporaries including Ulysses S. Grant and Robert E. Lee were distinguished combat leaders. He retired from the military partially on the belief that his lack of combat experience would retard his career.

When states began succeeding from the Union, Sherman resigned his position at the Academy and went to Washington D.C. to offer his services to the Union. He was not well received, and he went to St. Louis, where he became president of the St. Louis Railroad, which was a streetcar company. He held that position for only a few months before the Confederates fired on Ft. Sumpter. Sherman was called to Washington and was commissioned as a colonel in the 13th Infantry Division.

He was at the Battle of First Manassas on July 1, 1861 and was one of the few Union officers to perform with distinction. Early in the battle, he found and crossed an undefended ford and led a successful attack against the Confederate flank; *however*, later in the day, the Confederates counter attacked and the whole Union Army retreaded in disarray to Washington. Despite the defeat, Lincoln was impressed by Sherman and he was promoted to Brigadier General.

Sherman was stationed in Kentucky. The defeat at Manassas and the condition of the army in Kentucky so disillusioned Sherman that he contemplated suicide and insisted on being relieved of command. The press described him as insane.

By December 1861, Sherman had recovered sufficiently to return to duty, but he served in non-combat roles. He provided logistical support for Ulysses S. Grant in the capture of Fort Donelson in February 1862. During that campaign, he told Grant he had great faith in his leadership and offered to serve Grant in any way he could.

Sherman got his wish in March 1862 when he was assigned to serve under Grant in the Army of West Tennessee, where Sherman commanded the 5th Division. That Army was tested the following month at Shiloh. Sherman dismissed intelligence reports indicating that a large Confederate army commanded by Albert Sidney Johnston was about to attack. He made no defensive preparations for the attack that would begin the largest military engagement in the history of the Western Hemisphere. He apparently did not want to appear over alarmed because of the criticism of his performance in Kentucky. He wrote his wife that if he took more precautions "… they'd call me crazy again".

When the attack came on the morning of April 6, 1862, Sherman's army was caught unprepared. They were overrun, and the best that can be said of Sherman's performance is that he rallied his troops to conduct an orderly retreat. But the next day, Sherman was prominent in the Union counterattack that won the battle. Sherman was wounded twice and had three horses shot out from under him. Grant and Lincoln were so impressed with Sherman's performance that he was promoted to Major General.

After Shiloh, Grant's trust in Sherman increased. Over the following 18 months, Sherman participated in all of Grant's campaigns from Vicksburg to Chattanooga. Despite mixed results on the battlefield, Sherman had become Grant's most dependable lieutenant. Grant had more confidence in Sherman than Sherman had in himself. Sherman once said:

"I'm a damn site smarter than Grant. I know more about organization, supply and administration and about everything else than he does. But I'll tell you where he beats me and beats the world. He don't care a damn what the enemy does out of his sight. But it scares me like hell."

In the spring of 1864, Grant was transferred to Virginia to face Robert E. Lee's Army of Northern Virginia and to take command of all the Union Armies. Sherman succeeded to Grant's former position as head of the Army of the West. Sherman now commanded nearly 100,000 men, and he had to command them without relying on Grant's leadership.

Sherman rose to the task. He promptly invaded Georgia and headed toward Atlanta. On the way, he fought Confederate armies led by Joseph Johnston, who was considered by his superiors as overly cautious, and later John Bell Hood, who without question was overly aggressive. Sherman took Atlanta by forcing Hood to abandon the city on September 2, 1864. The victory made Sherman a household name in the Union and was instrumental in Lincoln's re-election in November of 1864.

After Atlanta, Sherman and Hood sparred with each other until Sherman persuaded his superiors to allow him to disengage from his lines of communication and supplies to attempt his March to the Sea. He told Grant he would conduct "hard war" and he would "Make Georgia howl".

Nothing like this had been attempted in military history. He led 62,000 men across Georgia with the goal of taking Savannah. His Army cut supply lines and lived off the land. It took only 40 days for Sherman to get to Savannah, leaving over $100,000,000 of damage behind. On December 21, 1864, Sherman famously telegraphed Lincoln giving the President Savannah as a Christmas present.

Sherman's accomplishment was so widely praised that a bill was introduced in Congress to promote Sherman to Grant's rank of Lieutenant General, with the thought that Sherman might replace Grant, who was thought by some politicians to be making insufficient progress against Lee. Sherman would have none of it. He said:

"General Grant is a great general. I know him well. He stood by me when I was crazy, and I stood by him when he was drunk; and now we stand by each other always."

After capturing Savannah, Sherman fought old foe Joseph Johnston through the Carolinas. Sherman advanced through swampy terrain on corduroy roads that his army built from felled trees at the rate of 12 miles per day. This achievement prompted Johnston to say: "… there has been no such army in existence since the days of Julius Caesar."

Although Robert E. Lee surrendered to Grant at Appomattox Court House on April 9, 1865, Sherman's war went on. Soon after Lee's surrender, Sherman entered negotiations for the surrender of Johnston's army. Johnston and Jefferson Davis insisted on favorable terms. Sherman eventually agreed to terms he believed to be consistent with those Grant had offered to Lee, but it didn't turn out that way.

Politicians in Washington, who were jockeying for power after Lee's surrender and Lincoln's assassination proclaimed Sherman's terms to be too generous and refused to approve them. Secretary of War Edward Stanton denounced Sherman publicly. Sherman nearly was removed from command. Eventually Johnston ended the issue by agreeing to surrender on April 26, 1865, under purely military terms.

In July 1866, Congress promoted Grant to a newly created rank of General of the Army, and Sherman was elevated to Lieutenant General. When Grant became president in 1869, Sherman was promoted to General of the Army, a position he held until he retired in November 1883.

After retirement, Sherman lived in New York City. He was proposed as a presidential candidate for the election of 1864, but famously declared "I will not accept if nominated and will not serve if elected."

Sherman died in New York on February 14, 1891. Confederate General Joseph Johnston served as an Honorary Pallbearer. He kept his hat off during the funeral as a sign of respect in the cold, rainy weather. Someone with concern for Johnston's health asked him to put his hat on, to which Johnston replied: "If I were in his place and he were standing here in mine, he would not put on his hat." Johnston caught a cold that day, which developed into pneumonia, and he died a few weeks later.

When Sherman died, the Pennsylvania Railroad provided a special train to transport his body to St. Louis. At 8:48 a.m., the train arrived at Union Depot, which was nearby the current St. Louis Amtrak Station. There was a Cavalry officer's Sabre slung across the locomotive's headlamp. The St. Louis Light Artillery fired a volley.

The casket was placed on a caisson drawn by four black horses and proceeded on 11th St. to Market Street, then North on 12th St. to Pine St. and Grand Ave., then for seven miles to the Calvary Cemetery on Florissant Ave. The casket was followed by a Cavalry escort, and a funeral procession of 12,000. There were veterans of Sherman's Army and other military units, including some from the Confederate Army that Sherman fought.

The four-hour procession ended at the Sherman family gravesite. His wife and two of his children already were buried there. Sherman's son Willie had died of typhoid fever while accompanying his father's Army after the surrender of Vicksburg. His son Charles died during the Savannah Campaign. Sherman had never met him. His wife Ellen had died in 1888.

It was a simple service. The casket was draped with flags, but there were no flowers. Sherman's son, the Reverend Thomas Sherman, presided. As the casket was lowered, the flags were removed and buglers from the 7th Cavalry played Taps. Volleys were fired over the grave followed by three artillery salvos from a nearby hill and the service was concluded.

Sherman's grave is just a few feet from today's Route 66. To get there, enter Calvary Cemetery from Florissant Ave. Go straight and bear left following the signs to Sections 17, 18 and 19. At that triangle go straight for about 50 yards. The gravesite is on the left in Section 17.

Here's another Old West story about events that occurred on territory that later became part of Route 66.

John Chisum and the Chisholm Trail

A COUPLE OF DAYS AGO I was on my way from Houston to Catoosa, Oklahoma to interview Blaine Davis, whose family owns the Blue Whale. I usually go through Dallas when headed that way, but I was going to hit the evening rush hour, so I used my GPS to find an alternate route. I found a great one. I got off of I-40 in Buffalo, Texas and headed to Palestine. From there I followed Texas Highway 19 all the way to Oklahoma, and I did not get on an Interstate highway until I was just outside of Tulsa. It was a beautiful country ride through hilly farmlands and some wonderful lakes.

This route took me through Paris, Texas, which is where New Mexico rancher John Chisum is buried. John Chisum started with a small spread along the Pecos River. His ranch eventually had over 100,000 head of cattle. He formed a partnership with Charles Goodnight and Oliver Loving. Goodnight owned the JA Ranch in the Texas Panhandle, which by many accounts was the largest cattle ranch in history. Oliver Loving was another cattle rancher. Together they formed the Goodnight-Loving Trail, which went from Fort Belnap, Texas through the Llano Estacado to Fort Sumner, New Mexico.

As an interesting aside, the death of Gus McRae in the Larry McMurtry book *Lonesome Dove* was based on the historic death of Oliver Loving. Loving was attacked and wounded by a band of Comanches while on a cattle drive. He escaped by floating down the Pecos River during a storm, and later died in Ft. Sumner, New Mexico after refusing to allow the amputation of his arm.

Chisum is known for his tangential participation in the Lincoln County War, which was a range war fought in 1878 in Lincoln County, New Mexico. The conflict was over the cattle and mercantile interests of James Dolan and Lawrence Murphy, who were trying to drive out English born John Tunstall, who had established a competing ranch and general store. Billy the Kid worked for Tunstall. Tunstall's murder and its aftermath gave rise to the legend of Billy the Kid.

John Chisum died on December 23, 1884, in Eureka Springs, Arkansas, while seeking the healing waters of the area to treat complications from surgery that removed a growth from his jaw. He was being transported home for burial, but wound up in Paris, Texas.

By now you must be wondering what this has to do with Route 66. The answer is Jesse Chisholm, who often is confused with John Chisum.

Jesse Chisholm was a mixed-blood Cherokee Indian for whom the Chisholm Trail was named. It was developed over several decades that preceded the cattle drives of the 1870s and 1880s. It started in 1826 as a trail to Wichita, Kansas that Jesse established for a gold seeking party. In 1830, Jesse later blazed a trail from Fort Gibson to Fort Towson, Kansas. These and other trails in which Jesse was involved became parts of the Chisholm Trail.

Its route during the cattle drive years is the subject of debate. Some historians claim it started in Donna, Texas or San Antonio, Texas. Others assert that no part of the Chisholm Trail was in Texas. They note that there is no evidence that Jesse Chisholm ever was in Texas, and that cattlemen of the day recognized that the Chisholm Trail started at Red River Station in Montague, County, Texas, where the trail crossed into Indian Territory (present day west-central Oklahoma). It went through present day El Reno, Duncan and Enid Oklahoma and crossed into Kansas at Caldwell. It originally ended in Abilene, Kansas. Newton, Wichita and Caldwell, Kansas all later served as the terminus of the Chisholm Trail.

Jesse Chisholm died in 1868 near the Route 66 town of Geary, Oklahoma and is buried there.

So, oddly enough, cattleman John Chisum never sent a cow up the Chisholm Trail, and Jesse Chisholm died nearly a decade before the first great cattle drive on the trail named for him.

Endnote: *Jesse Chisholm is buried near the Route 66 town of Geary. If you are near Geary and want to visit the gravesite:*

- *From Downtown Geary follow N 281 for about a mile and go right just before a curve in the road. If you take the curve you have gone too far.*
- *Go a few hundred yards and go left on N 2630.*
- *Go about four miles to a Stop Sign, then go right on E 910, which will be a gravel road.*
- *Go about two miles, cross a small Pony Bridge, then go left onto a gravel road (no road sign).*
- *Go left on E 980.*
- *Follow this road around a curve to the Jesse Chisholm Memorial Marker.*

The Memorial Marker is not the gravesite. Look to your left and walk down a small hill to the grave.

As remote a location as it is, the gravesite gets visitors. Every time I've visited there have been recently placed trinkets placed on the tombstone.

Since Billy the Kid died 45 years before Route 66 was commissioned, the connection with the Kid is tenuous. Still the Kid traveled to many places that became part of Route 66, and there must have been many people on Route 66 who would have known him. But all this really is just an excuse to write a story about Billy the Kid and the only known photos of him.

Billy the Kid on Route 66

A FEW NIGHTS AGO THE National Geographic Channel broadcast a show about a newly discovered photograph of Billy the Kid. If it's real, that would be a big deal because hitherto (that's for you Stevie Ray) there has been only one authenticated photograph of the Kid.

You must be thinking, what in the world does this have to do with Route 66? I must admit the connection is tenuous, but here goes.

The original 1926 alignment of Route 66 was created by connecting a series of existing roads to form a single pathway from Chicago to Los Angeles. Some of those roads went through parts of New Mexico that Billy the Kid was known to frequent. So, Billy the Kid traveled on roads that were incorporated into Route 66. Plus, when Route 66 was commissioned in 1926, Billy the Kid would have been only 65 years old, so there likely were people living along Route 66 who knew the Kid.

Admittedly, that's a thin connection for a Route 66 blog, but I have read a lot about Billy the Kid, and this gives me a chance to write about him. Here's the story.

Billy the Kid was born in Brooklyn, New York. When he was young his family moved west. Billy left home at an early age and wound up in Lincoln, New Mexico at the outbreak of the Lincoln County War. That conflict was a range war between James Dolan and Lawrence Murphy, who together had near monopoly on the local cattle and mercantile businesses, against John Tunstall, who was an Englishman who had come to Lincoln to start his own cattle and mercantile businesses. At the beginning of the war, Tunstall hired Billy and some other cowboys to protect his cattle from being stolen by the Dolan/Murphy faction.

Cattle rancher John Chisum had a tangential part in the Lincoln County War and was loosely aligned with Tunstall and Alexander McSween, who was Tunstall's lawyer and partner. Billy the Kid knew Chisum, and legend has it that Billy courted Chisum's niece Sally.

During the conflict, a posse of Dolan's men, including Lincoln County Sheriff William Brady, murdered Tunstall. Billy and other Tunstall employees formed a band known as the "Regulators" who were deputized by a local constable and given warrants to arrest Tunstall's murderers. The Regulators set out for revenge. As part of that revenge, they ambushed and killed Sheriff Brady and his deputy George Hindman on Lincoln's Main Street. Those killings put into motion the events that would lead to the legend of Billy the Kid.

The fight between the Regulators and the Dolan/Murphy faction continued on, and many people from both sides were killed. The culmination of the Lincoln County war occurred after a five day siege in which Dolan's men trapped several Regulators in McSween's house. The house eventually was set afire and McSween was killed. Billy the Kid escaped but was on the run.

New Mexico Territorial Governor Lew Wallace attempted to ease tensions in Lincoln Country by offering amnesty to anyone not under indictment. Billy was under indictment, but he was able to negotiate an amnesty in exchange for testifying in certain trials. Billy agreed to submit to a token arrest and testify, after which he was to be set free. But the district attorney, who was a Dolan/Murphy ally, refused to free the Kid. Billy and his best friend Tom O'Folliard escaped, and Billy spent the next 18 months on the run.

Billy eventually was captured. He was convicted of murdering Sheriff Brady, making him the only combatant in the Lincoln County War convicted of a crime. He was sentenced to hang.

While being held prisoner in the Lincoln County Jail, he engineered a daring escape during which he killed Deputies Bob Olinger and James Bell. Pat Garrett killed Billy the Kid three months later in Ft. Sumner, New Mexico. Pat Garrett authenticated the only known photograph of Billy the Kid before publishing it in his book *The Authentic Life of Billy, The Kid.*

Only known photograph of Billy the Kid

One hundred and twenty nine years later, a western photograph collector named Randy Guijarro bought three tintype photos for $2.00 from a shop in Fresno, California. He had no clue what was on them. One of the photos was a 4"x5" scene of 18 people playing croquet in front of a schoolhouse with some distinctive trees nearby. When Randy examined the photo under a loop, he found that one of the men looked like Billy the Kid.

The National Geographic Channel chronicled the process through which Randy attempted to have the photo authenticated.

Alleged new photograph of Billy the Kid

Randy first visited an expert to confirm that his photo was an actual tintype, which is a photograph made by putting an image on a thin piece of metal which is then coated with a lacquer to support the photo. The expert was able to use a chemical analysis to confirm that Randy's tintype was real, and that it was made during the time period in which Billy the Kid was in New Mexico.

Randy next visited a face recognition expert who provided substantial, but inconclusive, evidence that Billy the Kid was in the photo. Moreover, it appeared that Regulators Charlie Bowdre, Tom O'Folliard and Big Jim French also were in the photo, as well as John Chisum's niece Sally. They speculated that the picture may have been taken at Bowdre's wedding, because one of the women in the picture compared favorably with a known photo of Bowdre's wife.

Armed with this evidence, Randy took his picture to Brian Lebel, who had auctioned the photo that Pat Garrett identified as being of Billy the Kid for $2,300,000. Lebel was not impressed with Randy's photo. LaBelle said that he frequently was presented with photographs purporting to be of the Kid or other western figures, and they almost always were of other people. Part of his skepticism was based on the unlikely event that Billy the Kid and a bunch of Regulators would be playing croquet with Sally Chisum just when a photographer happened to be around. He said that more evidence would be needed to verify that the photo was of the Kid, and that neither he nor any other reputable dealer would handle it without 100% certainty as to its authenticity.

Randy took the picture to another dealer who showed some interest but affirmed that 100% certainty would be needed to authenticate the photo, and to get that certainty, all of the people in the picture would have to be identified and the exact location of the photo would have to be found. Randy set out to gather that evidence.

Randy next visited Paul Hutton at the University of New Mexico. Hutton is a well-known western historian who has appeared on many documentaries about the Old West. Hutton conceded that the photo looked like Billy, but he did not offer much encouragement on Randy's chances of getting the picture authenticated. But he told Randy that he might find some clues by reading Sally Chisum's diary.

The diary turned out to be a fragmentary document written in Sally's handwriting that was difficult to read. But the diary yielded a clue. She made reference to a visit from the Regulators at her Uncle John's ranch on a specific day in 1878. This was the first evidence that Sally knew the Regulators, thus raising the possibility that she might have appeared in a photo with them.

Armed with this new evidence, Randy hired a private investigator from Lincoln County to help him to find the location on John Chisum's ranch where the photo was taken. Randy and the investigator visited several local ranchers. They all said they had never seen any terrain like that shown in the picture in Lincoln County.

With this disappointing news in mind, Randy went to another facial recognition expert, this time one with expertise in computerized facial recognition technology. This expert concluded that the people in the photo almost certainly included Billy, Charlie Bowdre, Tom O'Folliard and Sally Chisum. Now Randy needed to try again to find the location where the picture was taken.

Randy's investigator eventually put him in touch with the owner of the ranch that John Tunstall had owned. The ranch had been in his family for five generations. He examined the photo and had a thought about where it might have been taken. Everyone went to the location, and the terrain looked similar to that in the photo; *however*, there was no school or trees resembling those in the photo. Still, it looked pretty close.

In a last ditch effort, Randy took his tintype to a numismatist who specialized in authenticating photographs. The numismatist was as skeptical as Brian Lebel had been. Nonetheless, he agreed to conduct his own due diligence.

In the closing scene of the National Geographic Channel show, Randy visited the numismatist's office to find his conclusions. The meeting took place on Friday, October 16, and the show was aired on October 19. The cool thing was that although much of the show appeared to be staged reenactments of previous events, the meeting with the numismatists was filmed live just three days before the show was aired. Randy's reactions to the results were not staged.

When Randy arrived, the numismatist and his assistant looked as skeptical as they had during their previous meeting. They told Randy that during the course of their due diligence investigation, they visited the site that the Tunstall Ranch owner had identified. They found a general match with the terrain in Randy's photo.

Then they put forth some surprising information. They found some wooden ruins where the schoolhouse in Randy's photo would have been. By using some computer modeling technology, they were able to reconstruct the structure, and it was a plausible match of the schoolhouse in Randy's photo.

Nonetheless, the experts said that matching the structure in the computer model to the structure in the photo was insufficient to authenticate the picture. They told Randy they had conducted additional due diligence with respect to the identities of the other people in the photo, including interviewing the facial recognition experts Randy had engaged. Randy appeared to be bracing himself for yet one more rejection.

At the conclusion of the numismatists' due diligence report, they told Randy that they had determined with 100% certainty that the photo was of Billy the Kid, and that's its value was $5,000,000. Three cheers for Randy and his tenacity in treating the world to this new piece of western lore, not to mention his new wealth.

Billy the Kid's grave is in Fort Sumner, NM less than an hour's drive off of Route 66. He is buried next to his best friend Tom O'Folliard and fellow Regulator Charlie Bowdre. There is a Billy the Kid Museum nearby. It's a worthwhile detour.

This is another story about events that happened in Route 66 towns before Route 66 was commissioned. It's about a still unsolved mystery that is kept in memory today by a Weatherford, Oklahoma motorcycle club which, unlike most MCs, admits women as members.

The Mystery of Dead Woman Crossing

A FEW DAYS AGO I WAS traveling on Route 66 between Catoosa and Weatherford, Oklahoma to film some interviews for the Pilot TV show I am producing about riding motorcycles on Route 66. Deb Mooney of Weatherford had planned to go on the ride I made in August between Chicago and Devil's Elbow to shoot footage for the Pilot, but she had to cancel at the last minute. So I arranged to interview Deb while I was in Weatherford. We agreed to meet for the interview at the original Lucille's, which was a Route 66 roadhouse and gas station in Hydro, Oklahoma that Lucille Hammons operated for 59 years.

Deb says she is a banker by day and a biker by night. She isn't kidding. Deb and her husband Perry ("Scooby") are members of the Iron Plainsmen Motorcycle Club. The MC has three chapters: Geronimo's Bluff; Moscow Flats; and Dead Woman's Crossing, in which Deb and Scooby are members.

It was raining when they rode up. Scooby was on a Heritage Softail and Deb was on a black Fatboy with ape hangers. I told her that riding in the rain to meet me for the interview was above and beyond the call of duty, and she replied "Well, you told me you wanted to get film of me on the bike."

I asked Deb about the meaning of "Dead Woman's Crossing." She told me that there are different versions of the story, all involving an unsolved murder and a haunted bridge near the Route 66 town of Weatherford, Oklahoma.

The version she understood to be true was a bit vague in detail. She said that back in the "stagecoach days," a woman was crossing a field with her baby near a bridge over Deer Creek. The baby died and in a fit of grief the woman killed herself. Deb was unsure whether the woman hung or shot herself. The bridge where all this happened became known as Dead Woman's Crossing. At night you are supposed to be able to hear the woman grieving the death of her child.

Another popular account is that the crossing originally was called Dead Woman's Bridge. In this version, a woman was crossing the bridge when her daughter fell out of a buggy and broke her neck. The mother then hung herself in grief. At night you are supposed to be able to hear the sounds of the buggy crossing the now haunted bridge.

In still another grizzly version, a woman was crossing the bridge with her baby when she was attacked. The woman was tied between two trees and her head was cut off. The baby was never found. Under this legend, at night the woman can be heard walking up and down the bridge searching for her head and her baby.

Here's the more likely story.

According to Wikipedia, a woman named Katie DeWitt James filed for divorce from her husband in 1905. The next day, Katie and her daughter Lulu Belle boarded a train in Custer City, Oklahoma. They were bound for Ripley to visit Katie's cousin. They never arrived.

A few weeks later Katie's father became concerned that he had not heard from her, and he hired an investigator to, well, investigate. The investigator found that Katie and her daughter got off the train in Weatherford in the company of a prostitute who lived in Clinton, Oklahoma. The next morning, the prostitute, Katie and her daughter left in a buggy. Two hours later the prostitute showed up back in Weatherford alone.

The investigator learned that Katie, the prostitute and the baby had been spotted near Deer Creek. He found the baby, who had been left with a stranger. The baby was unharmed but was covered in blood. The investigator found the prostitute in a nearby town. She denied killing Katie, but the prostitute killed herself with poison later the same day. Katie's decomposing body was found about a week later near Deer Creek. She had been shot in the head with a .38 caliber bullet and the head was found several feet from the rest of the body.

The bridge where all this happened has not existed since the 1980s, but a new bridge has been built nearby. The original bridge being gone, it's a bit unclear where you are supposed to go to experience any paranormal activity.

Deb's chapter of the Iron Plainsmen took their name from this legend. They help to maintain the new bridge. The chapter currently has 14 members, but they have several prospects in the pipeline. The Club does lots of fundraising, including sponsoring benefits for veterans organizations, breast cancer funds, Toys for Tots, Special Olympics and St Jude's Hospital. Although Deb is proud to be the only female full patch member, she is not selfish about it. She is working to get more women into the MC.

Martin Milner RIP

O*N THE FRIDAY NIGHT* of October 7, 1960, folks watching CBS television heard the snappy beat of a Nelson Riddle tune as their black-and-white screens showed a Corvette convertible cruising through a misty countryside as the words "Route 66" floated across the screen. The camera focused in on Martin Milner, who was driving, then George Maharis, who was trying to make sense of a map. They were on their way to Biloxi, Mississippi and were lost. Martin Milner asked "How did we get off of US 66? So began *Black November*, the first of 116 episodes of *Route 66* that aired over four seasons.

The show featured Todd Stiles, played by Martin Milner, and Buz Murdoch, played by George Maharis. Todd was the son of a formerly wealthy businessman who had died leaving Todd nothing but a Yale education and a new Corvette convertible. Buz was an edgy survivor of New York's Hell's Kitchen who had worked for Todd's father. The show chronicled Todd's and Buzz's adventures as they explored the United States in the Corvette taking odd jobs to pay their way.

Route 66 was unique in that it was shot entirely on location. Producer and writer Sterling Silliphant would travel with a location manager to find appropriate venues for filming. Silliphant would write the scripts as he traveled, and the production crew would arrive a week or so later to shoot the show.

Almost none of the episodes were on Route 66. But they captured the spirit not only of Route 66, but of America. It was a time of innocence and optimism now lost and largely forgotten.

John F. Kennedy was elected as our 35th president a month after the first episode aired. No one had heard of Vietnam. Martin Luther King had not yet risen to national attention. There was no internet, e-mail or cell phones. Nor was there a 24 hour news cycle; indeed, there were only three TV stations (and in our rural Connecticut house, we got only one of them). It was a time of opportunity and prosperity in which American audiences could understand a TV show about two young men traveling the heartland to find the country, and in the process, find themselves.

Marty Milner died of heart failure on September 6 at his Carlsbad, California home. He was 83.

Although many fans remember Marty for *Route66*, he had an impressive acting career both before and after his stint on the show. He was active from 1947 to 1997. In those 50 years he appeared in over 60 movies and scores of TV episodes.

His film debut was in the 1947 movie *Life with Father* with William Powell. He also was in *The Sands of Iwo Jima* with John Wayne in 1949 and in *Mr. Roberts* with Henry Fonda, Jimmy Cagney, William Powell and Jack Lemon in 1955. In 1957 he was in *The Sweet Smell of Success* with Burt Lancaster and Tony Curtis. That movie was loosely based on the life of Walter Winchell, and in some quarters is believed to have been the catalyst that ultimately led to Winchell's disgrace and loss of influence in journalism.

Before starring in *Route 66,* Milner appeared on many of TV shows, including recurring appearances in *Dragnet, The Life of Riley, Westinghouse Playhouse, The Millionaire* and *The Twilight Zone.* After *Route 66* was canceled, he played Officer Pete Malloy for seven seasons in the Jack Webb series *Adam 12*. He also appeared in *The Swiss Family Robinson*, *MacGyver* and *Murder She Wrote.*

He had a remarkable personal life. He met singer/actress Judith Jones at a Hollywood dinner party in 1956. They got married in 1957, had four children and remained married until his death.

Martin Milner starred in a TV show that had a relationship with Route 66 in name only. But it was a powerful show that can take us back to a simpler time when America was about to lose a good deal of its innocence but still was fresh. I often have the theme song to *Route 66* in my head and picture Todd and Buz in their Corvette as I ride across Route 66. I suspect I'm not the only one.

Stories from the Heart

These stories generally are not about Route 66, and some of them aren't even about riding motorcycles. But they are stories that are sometimes very personal and always close to my heart. Most of them are about friends who have passed away. I almost didn't publish some of them because I was not sure they were the kinds of stories my followers were used to seeing from me. But they turned out to be among the most popular of my stories.

This is the last photo of Tommy Cox and me. It was taken at an Ole Miss baseball game the year before he died. We pledged the Alpha Tau Omega Fraternity at Ole Miss together in August 1973 and were initiated into the Fraternity together in January 1974. We were roommates in the Fraternity House for two years. We went to jail together. He was best man at my wedding (well, the first one). We were friends until he died in Oxford, Mississippi on June 6, 2018. A 45 year friendship with memories that will be with me until I'm gone.

This is the story of the death of my life-long friend Tommy Cox. At Tommy's Celebration of Life, his wife Lisa quoted Dr. Seuss: "Don't cry because it's over. Be happy it happened." Of course, she was right. But I cannot read this story without shedding tears.

The Big Blink

In late May this year I flew to Corpus Christi to pick up a new Harley-Davidson Road Glide. It's battleship gray with a 107-inch engine, cruise control, a sound system with front and back speakers and a full tour pack. The 200-mile ride from Corpus to Houston was through perfect weather on a beast of a bike.

The next morning, I sent a text message to my Ole Miss ATΩ fraternity brother and lifelong friend Tommy Cox, who was ill, to see how he was doing. I got a response from his wife Lisa who told me Tommy had just been put into hospice care. Within the hour I was on my new motorcycle for the nine-hour ride to Oxford, Mississippi, to be with my friend when he died.

* * *

In February I had received a call from our fraternity brother Gerry Gafford. He told me that Tommy was sick and if I didn't visit him immediately I might not get another chance. I called Tommy, and he told me he had been diagnosed with inoperable throat cancer that had metastasized to his stomach. His condition was "inoperable but manageable".

The next week I rode to St. Louis to do some research for one of my Route 66 projects. I already had plans for that research, but the trip was an excuse to go to by Oxford to visit Tommy. After spending a day in St. Louis, I hopped on I-55 for the six-hour ride through Memphis and Sardis Lake to Oxford.

Tommy looked pretty good. He was unable to eat solid food, so he was being fed intravenously and he had lost weight, but he still was pushing 200 pounds. He said he had good days and bad days, and that most of them were pretty good.

He seemed well, and we talked about going to an Ole Miss baseball game that afternoon, but his energy didn't last. I could see he was getting tired, so I said my goodbyes after a visit that lasted about an hour. I left encouraged.

Over the next few months I found excuses to swing by Oxford. Toward the end of May, I stopped by Tommy's house on my way back from Chicago. This time, he was at home in a hospital bed. He had been having problems with medications that caused him to retain water. He had gained and lost over 30 pounds of water weight since I last had seen him.

There was no bigger sports fan than Tommy Cox, and he especially loved Ole Miss baseball. He also was a reader. I noticed that there was no TV, computer or books in his room and I asked how he was keeping up with sports. He told me that he hadn't been watching sports or reading during recent weeks. I asked how he was spending his time and he told me "I think about things." Those were the last words of substance he spoke to me.

He was scheduled to see his doctor the next day to discuss treatment options. I offered to stay to help him get to and from the doctor's office and he told me he'd let me know. I didn't hear from him the next morning, so I headed back to Houston with a feeling of confidence that the doctors would stabilize his recovery.

Two weeks later I was back in Oxford.

* * *

When I got to Tommy's room, the hospital had initiated what hospices do. All life-prolonging treatments had been discontinued and he was being medicated only to make him comfortable. He couldn't speak, but he knew his friends were there. If someone said something he could smile, and he could squeeze your hand to let you know he was still with you.

Only Tommy's closest friends knew he was in hospice, and they all came as soon as they could. I had come in from Houston. Malcolm Blaine, who had played golf tournaments against Tommy while they were in high school, came from Kentucky. David Chapman flew in from Florida. Gafford came from Atlanta. All his friends from the Oxford area came to visit. Tommy's room often was overflowing with his friends.

As time was getting short several clergymen visited. Our fraternity brother Shuler Griffin, much to my surprise, had become an Episcopal priest since the last time I'd seen him. A clergyman from inside the hospital visited to offer assistance and give condolences.

Finally, Duncan Gray, who had been Episcopal Bishop of Mississippi, came to administer the Sacrament of Holy Unction, which is the right of anointing the sick by the laying on of hands for the healing of the spirit, mind and body. It was explained to me as a ritual designed to separate Tommy's soul from his physical being, although I don't think that description is quite right.

Tommy, his wife Lisa, Bishop Gray, Malcolm, Molly Meisenheimer, who has been married to our fraternity brother Ed for 40 years, and I were the only participants. We held hands in a circle while Bishop Gray gave the sacrament.

I never had participated in anything like this. We all had to fight to keep our composure, but Bishop Gray was strong and helped us through it. At the time, it struck me that the service was as much to give the rest of us a sense of release and closure as it was to anoint Tommy. I'm sure that everybody else understood that before the service began. I found a respect for religious traditions that I had not considered previously.

I told Lisa that I had prayed more in the last three days than I had during the rest of my life cumulatively, and I wasn't exaggerating. It never occurred to me that my prayers would do anything for Tommy; *however*, I was surprised at the comfort they gave me. Perhaps that's something else I should consider more closely.

The next morning, I was at my hotel getting ready to go to the hospital when Lisa called to tell me Tommy had passed away. He died peacefully while he was alone with her. He had waited to have a private moment with her to let go.

Tommy didn't want a funeral. Instead he wanted his friends to gather for a celebration of life. That celebration was held in Oxford the month after he died. About 100 people RSVP'd to say that they would attend. Twice that many came.

* * *

I met Tommy Cox 45 years ago when we pledged the Alpha Tau Omega fraternity in August 1973. I blinked, and four and a half decades had passed. So, Tommy and I had 45 years of stories. Contrary to popular lore, most of them are suitable for polite society.

There were 44 members in our pledge class. Out of the 43 others, I don't recall how I came to be so close to Tommy in particular. It may have been as simple as our having similar senses of humor, playing cards and drinking inhuman amounts of beer together. Also, Tommy was smart.

Whatever it was, we spent lots of time together. I was from Haddam, Connecticut. It was hard for me to get home for school holidays, so I started spending them at Tommy's house in Gallatin, Tennessee. We won boatloads of money playing cards with Tommy's friend John Ketchrin, who was the second worst card player in history.

We were initiated into the fraternity in January 1974. Two months later we were in the Lafayette County Jail together after I Streaked Sorority Row in front of a couple of thousand Scarlet O'Hara's. He was the getaway driver, and we got away, only to be ratted out and arrested. He placed his one phone call to his mother.

We lived together in the "Old House" section of the fraternity house for two years. During that time, he visited me in Connecticut a few times. On one visit we drove his mother's giant Oldsmobile 225 (aka, the "Duce and a Quarter"). When we got out of the car in my parent's driveway, my mother gave him a big hug and said, " Sambo, it's so good to have you home." She had mistaken Tommy for me.

He was best man when I got married.

A decade and a half after graduating I called Tommy and told him I had just moved to Houston, had bought a car that would go 150 miles an hour, and I lived 300 miles from the Mexican border. He paused for a few seconds, then said, "I'm proud of you. It's been a long time since you came up with something like this." He flew to Houston the next day. We drove to Nuevo Laredo for international relations.

In recent years I enjoyed attending Ole Miss baseball with Tommy. Baseball is the perfect sport for catching up with friends because the game is so methodical that there is plenty of time to yak without missing the action. Those kinds of times define old friendships. There is a comfort between lifelong friends that does not need reaffirmation. It's just there.

* * *

We and our fraternity brothers spent our time sipping beer, playing cards, watching or playing sports, and plotting on how to get dates. If we got a date we spent our time scheming on how to get them into a close encounter of a frisky kind, which (except for Dave Tranberg) was an uncertain proposition. Thus, the need for more beer. We studied with whatever little time was left over.

Today, college students worry about "microaggressions." We didn't worry about microaggressions. We had uninhibited fun that would send today's college wimps into a lifetime of psychotherapy.

Tommy's bragging the night he lost his virginity, and providing physical evidence to corroborate his story, would send "Snowflakes" scattering to their safe spaces. He called his mother about that too.

Our fraternity brothers Frank Miller and Steve Wood's spin on the "Me Too" movement would have sent today's students trembling for the comfort of their service dogs.

Despite my impeccable reputation as a legal scholar, any one of a litany of things I did every day would preclude my survival of a Senate Supreme Court confirmation hearing.

Nonetheless, it was an innocent time, and we were innocent guys. We didn't do anything that young men in college hadn't been doing for as long as there have been young men in college. As the world has eased into moral relativism, we have retained most of that innocence.

All this was celebrated when we gathered to remember Tommy. It brought everyone back together, including a sprinkling of the aforementioned dates. Some of us hadn't seen each other in decades. Of course, everyone looked older. Years ago, people told me I looked like Nick Nolte. Today I get Colonel Sanders.

We had aged, but the light in everybody's eyes, the cuts of their smiles, their cackling laughter and their distinct voices all were the same. The afternoon was spent retelling old stories and laughing until it hurt. The evening was spent telling more old stories and laughing until we couldn't laugh any longer. By the time we were done there was no liquor left in Oxford. It was like we never had left the ATΩ house.

A couple of us were asked to say a few words, and we did. But Tommy's wife Lisa was the most eloquent. She spoke briefly with tears, a smile and love. She concluded by quoting, of all people, Dr. Seuss: "Don't cry because it's over, smile because it happened."

There were a lot of smiles that day as we remembered our friend.

* * *

It's been about three months since Tommy's celebration, and I've been back to Oxford for the funeral of another one of my fraternity brothers. Jim "Fat Jack" Jackson died of cancer. He had struggled with Parkinson's Disease for two decades, and he fought it with bravery and a cheerful outlook on life.

Hal "Neck" Griffith also died. Hal was tall, lean and strong. He had big ideas and made them happen. His self-confidence exploded like it came from a shotgun blast. In 1976, Hal organized our first fraternity formal in the New Orleans Super Dome, which had been open less than six months. He arranged private Amtrak cars to get us there and back. He became Road Manager for the Charlie Daniels Band. He was the worst card player in history. Hal died from years of substance abuse, and I'm glad I remember him the way he was.

* * *

Although 2018 has been a rough year, our group has been blessed that so few of us have been lost. Tommy's passing and the celebration of his life gave us the gift of renewing lifelong friendships and the gift of making us appreciate that we cannot squander our remaining tomorrows.

It's time for all of us to make new stories before I blink again.

* * *

A couple of years ago, I digitized a bunch of my Ole Miss photos and made them into a slideshow with the music we listened to back then. You can go to www.olemissato.com and can click on *Sam Allen's Happy Days Video* for about 20 minutes of 1970s nostalgia.

This is Sue Dailey, who was the only person I knew who owned a motorcycle before I bought my first one. She introduced me to David Cook, who's the guy in the photo with Sue, and I bought a Harley-Davidson Road King from him the next day. David was a swindler. He'd swindle you in the morning then pick up your bar tab that night. Everybody loved him, including me.

This is the story about buying my first motorcycle and about my friend David Cook who sold it to me.

Do you have any Gray Poupon?

I GOT A LOT OF POSITIVE feedback on last week's post about my first trip on Route 66 with Ricky Cook. Many subscribers, especially those from Houston, wanted to hear some stories about Ricky's father David. Here are a few. Better buckle up your seatbelts!

I bought my first motorcycle in December 1996. It was a 1995 Harley-Davidson Road King. I was driving my Corvette around Houston's 610 Loop and saw a billboard for Mancuso Harley-Davidson. I thought to myself that I could afford one of those. I called Sue Dailey, the only person I knew who owned a motorcycle, and Sue introduced me to David Cook. I bought the Road King from David the next day and we were friends from then on.

Being around David Cook was like being in an Elmore Leonard novel. There always were nefarious people around. Guys like "Gigolo Gene," who specialized in marrying wealthy elderly ladies and screwing around on them. There was "DC," who ran a biker bar and at age 66 went to prison for selling dope. Charlie G ran a flooring company that fronted for his book making business. There were plenty more.

David had a scam for everything. For $150 he would sell you a package that had a fake auto insurance card, an authentic handicapped parking tag, a press pass, an ordained minister's license and a variety of other credentials and forms of identification.

Once when the Astro's were in playing in the National League playoffs, David got us into the Astrodome parking lot by flashing his press pass. We parked in the front using his handicapped parking tag. The press pass got us into the Astrodome and then into the press box. The seats up there were great and there was a lot of free food and beer.

David ran a used car lot in Houston for years. He eventually closed the car lot and opened a motorcycle custom and repair shop called Luxury Cycles Unlimited.

David was a creative motorcycle shop owner, especially when it came to billing. It was not unusual for someone to drop a bike off for an oil change, and upon pick up, to find several hundred dollars of unordered parts and work. David would tell the customer that he put on the new parts and did the extra work because he knew the customer really wanted them anyway, and the customer rarely would complain.

Customers had to pay close attention to their invoices. Without care, they might miss the fact that they had been charged for the same part two or three times or charged for parts that were not put on the bike at all.

One of the easier things was getting a state inspection. David wouldn't bother with actually getting the bike inspected. Instead he would just buy a valid sticker from the inspection station across the street and add an extra convenience charge.

David would charge for work that never was done. One customer dropped his bike off at Luxury Cycles to get its heads "tubbed." That is a process in which the factory heads of a motorcycle are removed and a portion of them are filled in, leaving a small area roughly the shape of a bathtub, thus "tubbed" heads. The purpose is to get more compression and power. David had the heads on the customer's bike removed and told him that they had been sent out for the necessary machine work.

A couple of weeks later, the heads were back on the bike. David gave the customer a discounted deal on the price for the work. The customer was delighted with the discount and with his newly tubbed heads. He told everybody how great the bike was running and that he could especially feel a burst of power between second and third gears.

A year later, the customer was having problems with his engine, so he took the bike to Mancuso Harley-Davidson and asked them to take a look. He told Mancuso that the problem might be due to the increased compression he had because of having had the heads tubbed. Mancuso pulled the bike apart and told the customer that the heads had not been tubbed, and that his engine heads were the same as on any stock Harley.

But David's real talent was selling. David had a beautiful Fat Boy in his shop that he had been trying to sell for $25,000. The bike was worth the money. There were only 400 miles on it, and it was totally tricked out. It had a wonderful "Ghost Wolf" paint job that made the bike appear to be a solid deep black cherry color unless the sun shined on the tank in just the right way. When happened, a life-like Wolf with piercing yellow eyes would emerge from the undercoat.

One night, David and a bunch of guys, including me, hired a limo to hit some bars. We were so rowdy that the limousine was stopped by a police officer who threatened to arrest the driver and everybody in the limo. David talked the police out of arresting us. Later that night he told me he would sell me the Fat Boy for $20,500, but I had to buy the bike next day.

Suddenly, I understood. David did not own the bike. Instead, he was selling it for somebody else and got to keep everything over a $20,000 sales price, and David needed $500. I knew this was the cheapest David would be able to go, so I agreed to buy the bike.

The next morning, I gave David a cashier's check. He handed me the keys and told me I would get the title the next day.

Six months went by, and I still didn't have the title. I wasn't too worried about it because, after all, I had the bike. However, registration renewal was coming up, and I was worried I would need a title for the renewal. A few more months went by, so I called the Texas DOT to find out who owed the bike.

It was owned by David Osuch. I called Mr. Osuch and told him I expected we had a common friend named David Cook. Osuch said "Oh yeah; Cook's a great guy. I've known him for years! "Then I told Osuch that I had bought his Fat Boy and I still didn't have the title. Osuch said that was because Cook still hadn't paid all the purchase price.

Cook had told Osuch that when I bought the bike, I had only $10,000 in cash, that the rest of my assets were tied up in limited partnerships in England, and that it was going to take me 30 days to get liquid and pay the other ten grand. Osuch kept trying to get his money.

Cook finally told Osuch that I had been arrested for selling drugs, the DEA had confiscated the bike and I was in prison.

I headed to Floyd's Cajun Shack because I figured I would find Cook at the bar. Sure enough, he was there with a VO and Coke in hand. I told David that I had spoken with Osuch that afternoon. Cook said "Oh yeah; David's a great guy I've known him for years!"

Then I told him that Osuch had told me Cook had not paid for the bike. David didn't stumble. He told me I was right and started into a soliloquy justifying the lack of payment. After about a minute, David stopped talking and looked at me and said, "You want your title, don't you," and promised me I would get it the next day. Sure enough, I met David at Floyd's the next day, and I got the title. Who knows what money had to be shuffled around for David to come up with 10 Large overnight.

As an aside, I sold the Fat Boy two years later to someone in a purple Ford LTD who showed up with a green garbage bag with $23,000 in cash.

David liked to drink, and his drink of choice was VO and Coke. Late one night (or early one morning) David was pulled over by the police and David obviously had been drinking. The policeman asked David what a guy David's age was doing out drunk at that time of night?" David replied, "I'm on my paper route."

The next morning in the Harris County Jail when they were passing out the bologna sandwiches, David asked "Do you have any Gray Poupon?"

When David got out of jail the court ordered a Breathalyzer to be put on David's truck so he could not start it if he had been drinking. Some mornings, David would have so much alcohol in his bloodstream from the night before that he still couldn't start his truck. He would call me up and I would have to drive over from work and blow into the Breathalyzer to crank up the truck.

But the police are smart and knew people would try that kind of dodge. So, I would have to ride around Houston for 45 minutes or so until a beeper would go off signaling that the Breathalyzer had to be reactivated to keep the car moving. So, there I would be riding around in David's truck with my head down blowing into the Breathalyzer looking like I was blowing David. I probably was happier than Cook the day the Breathalyzer was removed.

There was no funeral when David died. Instead there was a party at the Hoffbrau Steak House, which had one of David's favorite bars. The place was overflowing. There was a microphone from which well-wishers could say a few words about David. I was at the bar with David's son Ricky and a friend of ours named Brett. Some woman we had never seen was at the microphone going on, and on and on.

I said "Who is this broad. This eulogy is longer than JFK's".

Brett replied "Yeah, and he screwed Marilyn Monroe."

No doubt David is resting in peace. I'm sure he conned his way through the Pearly Gates claiming he lent his soul to a friend who promised to drop it off in heaven the next week.

Endnote: *When David was in the hospital during his last days, friends told me that he had been asking to see me. I'd visited him in the hospital several times, and I couldn't imagine what important purpose he had in mind for this particular visit.*

I went to his hospital room and he said. "Sambo, I'm so glad you came. There's something I want to talk about with you. Do you know that display case in my shop with all that sports memorabilia? I'll sell it all to you at a great price!"

That was the last time I saw David.

This photo of Carrol Kelly and me was taken on Bear Tooth Pass in southern Montana in June 1996. It was on a motorcycle ride from Deadwood, South Dakota at the Sturgis Black Hills Motorcycle Rally back to Houston. It was the first cross country motorcycle ride for each of us. Carroll was an original member of the Deacons of Deadwood Motorcycle Club, which I founded in 2002. We rode tens of thousands of miles together before he died of cancer in 2008. I gave a framed copy of this photo to each Member of the Deacons of Deadwood at a celebration of his life we had following his funeral.

This is the story of how I met Carroll Kelly and our first motorcycle ride together, our last motorcycle ride together and lots of friendship in between.

Carousing with Carroll Kelly

In the spring of 1996, I was having dinner in the original small dining room at Ninfa's Mexican Restaurant in Houston with a hot long-legged blond who later would be my third, and last, ex-wife. A gangly guy came and sat at my table uninvited and introduced himself as Carroll Kelly.

Carroll said, "Is that your bike outside?" I said that it was.

Carroll continued: "I've got a bike."

I replied, "Good for you," and thought to myself who is this guy and why won't he go away?

Carroll asked if I had ever been to the Sturgis Motorcycle Rally. I told him that I had not been, but I planned to go in a few weeks. I really wished this guy would take off. He was interfering with my getting the hot blond into the sack.

Carroll asked, "Can I go?"

By this time, I was getting annoyed, and I replied "It's a free country. You can go wherever you want."

Carroll was persistent, and I wound up telling him that I knew a guy named David Cook who was trying to arrange a room for me at Sturgis and that maybe David could find a room for him too.

David and his crew always stayed at the Bullock Hotel in Deadwood, South Dakota, for the Rally. Deadwood is the town where Wild Bill Hickok was killed in Saloon No.10 by Jack McCall on August 2, 1876. David got us rooms, but not at the Bullock. Instead, we were at a Best Western at the edge of town, and only for only the Friday and Saturday nights at the beginning of the Rally.

Carroll and I shipped our bikes to Rapid City, South Dakota and flew up to get them. During our two days at the Rally, we rode with

David Cook and his Houston contingent to see Mount Rushmore and through Custer Park and the Needles Highway. At night we drank whiskey and played poker at Saloon No. 10.

On Sunday morning, Carroll and I started back to Houston. This was an adventure for each of us because neither of us had ever ridden across the country. I had been riding my Road King for less than six months, and Carroll's bike was an ancient Ultra Classic that leaked oil as fast as it could be poured in.

The goal on the first day was Billings, Montana. The ride was hard. There was a crosswind so strong that Carroll and I had to ride on the shoulder of the road and lean our bikes into the wind to avoid being blown over. The windshield on my bike blew off.

The next day we planned to ride over Bear Tooth Pass, through Yellowstone and then to Jackson Hole, Wyoming. This ride was even rougher than the day before. It was August, but it was snowing on the top of the Pass. Carroll and had our picture taken in a snow drift near the summit.

When coming off Bear Tooth Pass, we came to Silvergate, Montana, which was only about a mile outside of Yellowstone. Carroll and I were so cold we didn't think about continuing to Jackson Hole. Instead, we checked into the Range Rider Lodge, which was a large log building that once had been a gambling hall and whorehouse. Guests stay in the whores' old rooms, which still have their names on the doors.

The rate was $38 payable in cash. When we were checking in, we noticed a bar that was about 40 feet passed a locked gate at the entrance of the Lodge. I asked the check in guy what time the bar opened, and he said usually at 5:00, but he would open it for us right away. We made good use of their limited selection of brown liquor.

Carroll and I made it to Jackson Hole the next day, stayed two days then headed toward Colorado. About halfway there we stopped at a service station that had about 30 Hells Angels gassing up. Carroll was an outgoing guy, but sometimes he didn't know when to keep to himself. He strode up to one of the Angels and asked whether the AJs were going to Jackson Hole.

The AJ: "We ain't going to Jackson Hole."

Carroll persisted, telling the guy that Jackson was a great place just down the road, and that the Angles should check it out. The Angels made it clear that they were not going to Jackson Fucking Hole, and that Carroll had better Shut the Fuck Up and leave the Angels the Fuck alone, which wisely, he did.

It had been another windy day, and by the time Carroll and I got to Pueblo, Colorado, we were exhausted. I fell asleep with my jacket and chaps on. The next morning, I got a call from my office, and found I was going to have to spend a half a day working before I could leave. Carroll said he didn't have time to wait around and that he was heading home. Carroll rode that leaky Ultra all the way back to Texas, with a stop in Tombstone, Arizona.

Years later, Carroll wrote an account of this trip and posted it on my motorcycle club's website. Carroll's recollections about our meeting and that first ride are not quite the same as mine, but they are close. It was a lovely article that I value deeply. The story immediately following this one is about the article Carroll wrote.

By the next year, Carroll and I had become good friends of David Cook, and he got us rooms at the Bullock Hotel for the Rally. Carroll had recently married a classy chick named Jane who raised miniature horses. Carroll told everybody that Jane was flying to Sturgis, and he was going to meet her there.

When our group gathered to leave for Sturgis, Carroll showed up with his girlfriend Ann. I asked Carroll what he was going to do with Ann when his wife showed up. Carroll said it was no problem. He had an extra room for Ann down the hall.

That gambit worked out predictably.

One afternoon a group was in the bar at the Bullock and my date Tonya was looking for her reading glasses so she could read the menu. She asked, "Where are my cheaters?"

At that moment, Carroll and Ann were walking into the bar. Ricky Cook pointed to them and said, "There they are!"

Later in the week one of the guys in our group was going to his room and saw Ann drunk and in tears in the hallway. He went to see if he could help her, and she said she couldn't find her room key. About this time Carroll bee bopped through with his wife, who said "What's wrong Ann, can't find your keys?"

After Carroll and his wife passed by, the guy asked Ann if she had looked in her back pocket for her key. Sure enough, that's where it was. She thanked the guy and tried to show her appreciation by offering up a quickie that she said would take only 12 minutes. The guy said that he only had 10 minutes and left her in the hallway.

By the time Carroll got back to Houston divorce papers had been served.

By the middle of 2008, Carroll Kelly's had been diagnosed with cancer, and things were coming to finality. Outwardly, he looked good, and he did not talk about his health issues; *however*, some of his closest friends knew that his doctors had informed him that he had weeks, rather than months or years to live.

Our friend John Aubrey organized a motorcycle ride from Seattle back to Houston that we all suspected would be Carroll's last long ride. Eight of us went, including Ann.

John planned a great route. We stayed on the Pacific Coast Highway as much as possible until just north of San Francisco. The first couple of days were chilly, windy and misty, but the ride went through some magnificent countryside and along beautiful coastline. Early one evening we came across a large herd of elk in the middle of a redwood forest. The elk were right next to the road and were not scared of us.

From just north of San Francisco, we cut across the mountains to Reno, Nevada. From Reno, we rode 325 miles to Ely, Nevada, across Nevada's Highway 50, known as the "Loneliest Road in America." From Ely, the ride was across northern Utah to Grand Junction, Colorado, then through the mountains south to Cuchara, Colorado. From Cuchara, it was to Amarillo, Fort Worth and back to Houston.

During this ride, Tiger Woods was fighting it out with Rocco Mediate for golf's U.S. Open title. John, Carroll and I all followed the tournament during the ride home. We made it to the Stockyards Hotel Bar in Fort Worth in time to watch the Sunday round. At the end of the round Tiger and Rocco were tied, which meant the next day they would have to play 18 additional holes in a playoff.

Monday morning, we headed for Houston. I was listening to the U.S. Open playoff on the radio on my Ultra Classic. That's what all the bad ass bikers were listening to on their satellite radios that day. Carroll was leading the group, and just south of Dallas, he unexpectedly crossed about three lanes of traffic and exited I-45. I knew I couldn't get over in time, so I kept riding as I watched Carroll go down the exit ramp. It was the last time I saw Carroll on a motorcycle.

Carroll died on September 6, 2008. He had just finished playing golf with friends and was on his way to watch his grandson play little league football. He felt a little lightheaded and stopped into a drugstore for some medication. A few minutes later he was found dead beside his car. Carroll lived his life doing what he wanted to do right up until the moment he died

Carol was one of the original members of the Deacons of Deadwood Motorcycle Club, which I founded in 2002. Carroll was our first member to die, and we were uncertain on whether we should go to the funeral in our Colors or whether we should dress more traditionally. Carroll's family solved the problem by asking that we ride our bikes to the funeral in our Colors. They reserved a section of the church for us. A Deacon commented that the reserved seating was a nice gesture. I replied that just want to keep us way from the respectable people.

After the funeral, the Deacons rode in a procession to Ninfa's restaurant, where I had reserved the room where Carroll had introduced himself to me nearly a decade earlier. Carroll loved nachos, and I ordered all the nachos, beer and margaritas the Deacons could eat and drink. I also distributed framed copies of the photo of Carroll and me in the snow drift atop Bear Tooth Pass on our first trip to Sturgis.

Carroll would have liked our celebration of his life.

This story is about an article my friend Carroll Kelly wrote about me while he was a member of the Deacons of Deadwood Motorcycle Club. He wrote it in around 2005, and I published years later it as one of the blogs I was writing about Route 66 and riding motorcycles across the country. The blog did not come out until after Carroll had died.

Carroll could drive me crazy, but he was a friend who is missed. I wish he was still around; I know he'd have enjoyed this collection of stories (although I'm equally sure he would have been vocal about its shortcomings!).

Remembrances of a Friendship

My last blog had several stories about my friend Carroll Kelly. I had an enthusiastic response from folks who knew Carroll as well as from readers who never knew him.

In that blog, I told the story of how I met Carroll at Ninfa's Restaurant in Houston and our first ride to the Sturgis Motorcycle Rally. In telling that story, I mentioned that Carroll had written an article about those same events, and that although his recollections were a bit different than mine, they were pretty close.

Carroll was a founding member of a motorcycle club I founded in 2002 called The Deacons of Deadwood MC. Carroll's article came about through a program we once had under which the members at our monthly meetings would draw lots, and the winner (loser?) was required to write an article about an experience of his choice as a Deacon. Carroll wrote about the same events I related in my last blog posting. I thought it might be fun for my blog followers to see the article Carroll wrote about our meeting.

Carroll's article follows. It has not been edited other than formatting.

So, here it is.

"AN UNFORGETTABLE CHARACTER"
By Carroll Kelly – AKA "Speedy"

I know most of you are aware that the Readers Digest has, for many years, featured an article in its monthly publication entitled "The Most Unforgettable Character I Ever Met." I was never given the opportunity to write an essay in Readers Digest, but obviously, I have been given the privilege and task of writing an article for our Club's website, and I am titling my essay – – – "An Unforgettable Character."

This story begins in 1995 when I approached a strapping young man at Ninfa's Restaurant on Navigation. I asked this fellow if the motorcycle outside was his. He reluctantly admitted to the ownership of the bike. I related to him that I also owned a motorcycle and further, inquired as to whether or not he might be going to Sturgis, South Dakota in August. He responded by a statement along the lines of "yes, but what's it to you?"

Notwithstanding his unfriendliness, I forged ahead. He then related to me that he and a "large group" of people would be going to Sturgis. I asked him if I might include myself in that "large group" of people. He said, "Well I guess you can if you insist." At any rate, I got this fellow's name and phone number and early the next week I called him to attempt to move forward with this trip that would include several bikes and multiple riders. The fellow finally seemed reconciled to the fact that I was going to make this trip to Sturgis with him and his group of friends.

As things progressed it became apparent that the only people that were going on this trip in this context were this fellow that I met at Ninfa's and me. The "large group" obviously dissipated to he and I. As the trip grew closer to its beginning, we were making plans to have our bikes shipped, fly to Rapid City, South Dakota, pick up our bikes, and begin the odyssey in and around Rapid City, Sturgis, Deadwood, etc.

I soon learned that the "large group" of people that this fellow was talking about were people who, likewise, hauled their motorcycles to the Sturgis area, stayed in Deadwood, and casually rode around the area sightseeing, viewing ladies in scantily clad outfits, and hanging around the bars in the area acting like Macho Bikers.

My new friend and I met David Cook, the GURU of Deadwood at that time, and his entourage of bikers at the Bullock Hotel in Deadwood, South Dakota. Needless to say, David Cook did not have rooms for my new friend and me. So, we stayed at a third-rate motel on the outskirts of Deadwood, but were accepted into the David Cook group at the Bullock Hotel for refreshments, food, general BS, etc.

Those activities went on for several days and at the conclusion of the time in Deadwood, David Cook and his entourage loaded their classic motorcycles into their trailers and headed back to Houston. My new friend and I, however, undertook to return to Houston by taking a rather circuitous route through the Little Big Horn Battlefield; Billings, Montana; Bear Tooth Mountain; the Range Rider Hotel at the entrance to Yellowstone National Park; Yellowstone National Park; Jackson Hole, Wyoming; Cheyenne, Wyoming; Denver, Colorado; and points south. By this time my friend and I were on rather friendly terms and both of us seemed to be enjoying the trip, the sights, the food, and the camaraderie.

My friend did, and has developed, a habit of somewhat narcissistically taking times on many of the mornings of the trip to work on various projects from his hotel room with his office in Houston. During those times, I would twiddle my thumbs in my room and wait for my friend to finish his work so that we could continue our trip.

About 8 days into the trip, and on a Sunday evening, we located a lively biker bar in Pueblo, Colorado. After food and drinks, we returned to our respective rooms and I was told by my friend that we would not be able to leave the next day until sometime in the afternoon since he planned to work from his room in Pueblo with his office in Houston. We went to bed.

During the night I decided that the camaraderie, fellowship, and adventure of the trip to-date had been enough for me. I decided to tell my friend the next morning that I was going to mount my 1980 Shovelhead Harley (which, by the way, used about as much oil as it did gasoline on the trip) and take out on my own for Houston. This is what I did and my friend continued his trip through Albuquerque and Santa Fe, New Mexico; Tombstone, Arizona; and points south and west.

This trip was my first motorcycle trip, and I also learned it was my friend's first motorcycle trip of any significance. We would travel as much as 300 miles a day and would be totally exhausted from the day's activities.

As many of you know, my friend and I have now ridden together over 40,000 miles, and on many days we have covered 700 to a 1,000 miles a day. So, we have learned to be better bikers with much more stamina and know-how concerning the handling and manipulation of an 800 lb. motorcycle. All of the trips we have taken together have been wonderful, but this first trip was obviously a learning experience for both my friend and me.

At any rate, I made it home safely in about a day and a half from Pueblo, Colorado; and my friend made it home safely to Houston in about four more days of sightseeing and riding.

As we all know, in the world of Harley Davidson Motorcycles, it is "not the destination but the journey that counts." This trip was, of course, a wonderful experience for me. I met many interesting and friendly people and because of my friend's generosity, I was included in this, my first trip to Sturgis.

I know today that this trip with my new friend was one of the reasons for his idea, along with Ricky and David Cook, to form a motorcycle club in Houston that would be named the Deacons of Deadwood. Through my friend's hard work, this Club was formed. I am honored to be one of the founders of the Club. If you have not guessed by now – my new friend was and is "SAM ALLEN."

As I have stated previously, Sam and I have, with others, traveled across this Country and Canada on our motorcycles together. Those trips have also been unforgettable, but I know without Sam's leadership and tenacity, that many of the trips would not have taken place and that in all probability, the Deacons of Deadwood Motorcycle Club would never have been founded. It now has a membership of well over 50 members, has generated several hundred thousand dollars for charity, and has given me the opportunity to meet and become friends with other "unforgettable characters."

"Thanks Sam"

Endnote: *"Thanks Carroll"*

This is a story of a long ride I took during which I saw a total eclipse of the sun and later rode with some friends over the rainbow. It's a story of what riding motorcycles across the country is all about.

Beyond the Rainbow

RIDING MOTORCYCLES HAS an edgy glamour to it. Motorcycles erupt noise, vibrations and power. For guys barhopping or taking a weekend out of town ride, it's a testosterone mainline injection. Men who may work in offices during the day become invincible bad ass bikers as soon as they fire up their engines. When they roll into a bar, they're sure there is no man reckless enough to mess with them and there is no woman who can't be had.

Women get to dress in short shorts and halter tops. In cooler times, they get to wear skintight leathers often designed more to show off their bodies than keep them warm. They get to feel the vibration of a big V-Twin engine between their legs. They can strut their bodies as they ride from bar to bar. If they are not with a guy, no worries; there always is a back seat for a hot chick.

The problem for weekend warriors is that when the weekend ends, the bikes get parked, and the noise, vibration, power, short shorts, halter tops and leathers are gone. It's back to work until the next weekend ride.

But riding a motorcycle across the country is not a weekend thing. It's different and it's not for everybody. Anyone who rides across the country once finds out pretty quickly if they like it. Most don't. Some get scared. Many don't like being in the elements because bikers do not ride through the environment; they ride in it. The wind, rain, heat and cold beat you up over time and can be exhausting. Others get bored spending hours on the road.

But for those who love cross country rides, all those negatives are positives. The excitement comes not from the noise or power of the motorcycle, but from the unexpected. It can be a bit scary to head out across unknown country with no definite plans. But wariness of the unknown and battling the elements are all part of the adventure. Traveling for hours on secondary roads through towns hidden by the interstate highways that have bypassed them is special. Most of all, it's a solitary thing, and despite the noise of the engine and the effect of the elements, there is a peacefulness about it.

I do most of my cross country riding alone. Sometimes I travel with a group, but group riding really is several people riding alone. That's because there are no conversations except when stopping for gas or food or at the end of the day. Riding a motorcycle for 10 hours a day for a couple of weeks leaves lots of time for reflection, so long distance riders need to be comfortable with themselves and their inner thoughts. Sometimes I worry that I like the solitude too much, but there is no escaping that it's part of my essence.

I started my current ride a little over two weeks ago. I went from Corpus Christi, Texas to Oklahoma City, then rode the old Route 66 to its original 1926 terminus on the corner of 7th Street and Broadway in the Los Angeles Historic District. I hit 'R Place in Pasadena, California, which is my favorite Route 66 bar, then stayed at the Wigwam Motel in Rialto, where every room is its own giant concrete Tee Pee. From there, I headed across the Mojave Desert through Las Vegas to Provo, Utah, where I watched the total eclipse of the sun.

The eclipse was as magnificent as it was supposed to be. Of course, I hadn't bothered to buy the special glasses needed to view it safely. But folks at my hotel had plenty and lent me a set. As the eclipse approached fullness, things got darker, but like dusk rather than nighttime. The temperature went down at least 10 degrees. It lasted only a few minutes, but those minutes were worth experiencing. The next total solar eclipse in the United States will be in 2025 in Texas, and the next one after that won't be for 38 years from now. So realistically I have only one more chance to see another full solar eclipse during my lifetime.

After the eclipse, I went to Jackson Hole, Wyoming to meet two couples from Texas who had never been to Yellowstone. I had promised I'd take them through the park before heading home to Texas. It turned out to be a hard, tedious ride, but with a once in a lifetime experience toward the end.

The ride through Yellowstone was a series of misadventures that began before we got out of Jackson. We had planned to leave around 8:30 in the morning and I showed up at the appointed time. But one of the couples wasn't out of bed yet. It was 9:30 before we headed out. Then one of the group had a worry about tire pressure that took another hour to resolve. All that was OK, and we finally headed toward Yellowstone at 10:30.

The south gate of Yellowstone is only about 50 miles from Jackson, and it's about another 50 miles to Old Faithful. It usually is about a 90-minute ride. It was a glorious day for riding; sunny and 60 degrees when we started. Cold enough for jackets and chaps, but not so cold as to be uncomfortable. The ride was perfect until we got about two miles outside the gates of Yellowstone, where traffic came to a standstill. It took us over an hour to go those last two miles. One of the bikes over heated, so the two other bikes went into the park and waited for the last rider to catch up.

Then things got worse. It turned out that there was road construction going on all over the park. We would ride for 10 minutes then have a 20-minute stand still. This went on almost all the way to Old Faithful. The result: we arrived at 2:30. Four hours later than planned.

We tried to have lunch in the main dining room at the Old Faithful Inn, which is the largest log building in the world. Unfortunately, it closed for lunch five minutes before we got there. So, we went to eat in the bar. Old Faithful was scheduled to go off before our food arrived, so those of us who had never seen it went to watch and then came back to cold food. The waitress was nice enough to reheat everything.

After lunch, the plan was to go to Yellowstone Falls, which are in the yellow stone canyon that gives the park its name. The falls are three times higher than Niagara Falls (but not nearly as wide). That plan didn't work out. There was more road construction, much of it over gravel roadway that was hard to navigate on motorcycles. We decided to skip the Falls because we still had 95 miles to go to get out of the park to Cooke City, Montana, where we were going to stay that night.

There was not much daylight left by the time we had passed through the construction and found ourselves in the Lamar Valley heading toward the Northeast exit of the park. We saw some large buffalo herds (no, they were not bison; as soon as I start reading legends about Bison Bill I'll start referring to buffalos as bison). We hit a spat of rain, and I was determined to ride through it because I didn't think it would last long and because I was worried that if we didn't hustle through the remaining 60 miles to Cooke City we might wind up riding in the dark, which would not be wise in an area where the buffalo were roaming.

But I was traveling with a group and they wanted to put on their rain suits. So, we pulled into a large gravel truck maintenance area that was down a small hill. As we pulled in an exceptionally bright rainbow appeared just ahead of us. You'd think it would have made me think of the song *Somewhere Over the Rainbow*, but instead I thought about Johnny Mercer's lyrics to Henry Mancini's song *Moon River*:

> *Moon River, wider than a mile.*
> *I'm crossing you in style someday.*
> *Dream maker, you heart breaker.*
> *Wherever you're going I'm going that way.*
> *Two drifters, off to see the world.*
> *There's such a lot of world to see.*
> *We're after that same rainbow's end.*
> *Waiting 'round the bend.*
> *My huckleberry friend, Moon River and me.*

As I suspected, by the time everybody got their rain suits on the rain had almost stopped. We got on our bikes and rode up the hill. The moment we got onto the road; we saw the rainbow touching the ground no more than 30 yards ahead of us. There were no leprechauns and there was no pot of gold, so I figured that this must have been the beginning of the rainbow rather than the end. A moment later we had driven under our rainbow, so we literally were "Somewhere over the rainbow… where the dreams that you dare to dream really do come true".

Seeing the total eclipse of the sun was an experience, but not unique. Millions had seen it as it passed across the United States, and tens of millions had seen it on television and other media. But *that* rainbow belongs to only the five of us, and we'll have its beauty with us the rest of our lives.

I guess that at least a portion of me is a drifter off to see the world.

This photo of my friends Stevie Ray Skelton and Kim McMillen was taken at the top of Bear Tooth Pass in southern Montana the day after we literally rode somewhere over the rainbow.

This is a story about a ride I took to the Indianapolis 500 just before the 75*th* anniversary of D-Day and some thoughts I had about the young men who have fought in wars to keep us free. If you are "woke" I suggest you skip to the next story.

This one goes out to my friends Rhon and Lori Tranberg, who have hosted me at the "Race" for decades.

Respecting our Heroes at the Greatest Spectacle in Racing

IN THE PRE-DAWN HOURS 75 years ago today, 20,000 paratroopers, primarily from the United States' elite 82nd and 101st Airborne Divisions, parachuted into heavily defended German territory behind the five beaches on France's Normandy coast codenamed Utah, Omaha, Sword, Gold and Juno. It was H-Hour of D-Day. Their mission was to capture German artillery positions that could be used against the 165,000 soldiers who three hours later would embark from over 6,000 ships to charge those beaches, and to secure the transportation networks that would allow those soldiers to begin the inland invasion of France with the object of defeating the German Army during the Second World War.

The Normandy Invasion was supposed to have been launched the day before, on June 5, 1944. Bad weather caused the invasion to be postponed for a day. Because of the scheduled tides, postponement for an additional day would have put the mission off for at least another month. Supreme Allied Commander Dwight Eisenhauer ordered the invasion to be launched on June 6 even though the weather still was threatening.

With the exception of specially trained Army Rangers tasked with scaling the cliffs at Pointe du Hoc to capture enemy artillery positioned on the highest point between Utah and Omaha Beaches, none of the soldiers who participated in the Normandy Invasion had been in combat before. Casualties were feared to be as high as 50%, and the Allied commanders believed that experienced combat veterans would refuse to make the attack.

Ike had two speeches in his pocket: one announcing success, the other announcing failure and his taking personal responsibility for that failure. As D-Day progressed, it was uncertain which speech he would give.

Of course, D-Day was a success. Paris would be liberated 80 days later. Hitler would be dead, and the German Army defeated in less than a year.

* * *

The day before my brother Ted's 19th birthday he was home in Connecticut after completing Army infantry basic training. He ran into our father's law partner Chester Dzialo (pronounced Da zah lo), who saw from the insignia on Ted's uniform that Ted was in the same infantry division in which Mr. Dzialo had served during World War II. Mr. Dzialo took Ted to lunch. Conversation naturally led to military matters. Ted knew Mr. Dzialo had won a Silver Star on D-Day, and Ted was hoping to hear the story. Here's the story he told.

After the Japanese attack on Pearl Harbor, 17-year old Chester Dzialo and his best friend dropped out of high school and enlisted in the Army together. They were sent to basic training at different locations, and they lost track of each other.

Mr. Dzialo was on Utah Beach on D-Day. While under heavy enemy fire, he jumped into an artillery shell crater and landed on top of a GI he presumed to be dead. The GI was alive and turned out to be the friend with whom he had enlisted. They spoke for a few minutes until a Sargent came by and ordered them to move up. They did. Mr. Dzialo did not see his friend again until after the war. Amazingly, not only had both of them survived, neither had been wounded.

Ted asked Mr. Dzialo about the Silver Star. Mr. Dzialo did not sob but tears immediately welled in his eyes, and soon the tears were running down his cheeks. He told Ted that the citation he received along with the Medal stated that the award was being given due to conspicuous bravery in the face of enemy fire. He said he had not been brave that day; he had been scared shitless. This was the only time that anyone in our family ever heard Mr. Dzialo use profanity. He told Ted that he had long thought he should return the Medal and citation because he felt like a fraud for having received them.

Ted told Mr. Dzialo that he didn't think anybody would begrudge his keeping the Medal. Mr. Dzialo replied "Well, then that's OK." Mr. Dzialo did not tell Ted what he had done to earn the Medal.

Chester Dzialo and hundreds of thousands of young men like him from the United States, England, France, Canada, Australia and the other 15 countries comprising the Allied Forces in World War II saved the world from a tyranny that would be unimaginable given the manifest evil witnessed upon the liberation of Auschwitz, Bergen-Belsen, Dachau and other concentration camps.

My reverence for these brave young men always has been so profound I have difficulty discussing it in an even voice; I must resort to writing.

* * *

On the Sunday of Memorial Day Weekend each year over 300,000 people from the Heartland of America assemble at the Indianapolis Motor Speedway to watch the Indianapolis 500: The Greatest Spectacle in Racing.

The Race is a genuine Middle America event. Although there is plenty of rowdiness (witness the "Snake Pit" in the infield on turn three), by and large, the fans are well dressed and well behaved. By the end of the Race they also are well oiled.

When I went to my first Race in the 1980s, beer was not sold at the Speedway. Patrons were allowed to bring in coolers that would slide under the bleacher-style seats. I'm here to tell you that those coolers held exactly 22 beers. If someone wanted to bring in extra beer or food, they could bring in larger coolers that they would leave underneath the stands. No one would steal anybody's stuff.

This year I rode my motorcycle over 1,200 miles from Houston to Indianapolis for the Race. I stayed with my friends Rhon and Lori Tranburg, who have been gracious enough to host me many times over nearly four (not a typo) decades. Altogether, there were nine of us going to the Race. I had tail gated with some of them for years.

The weather forecast was 94% chances of rain. Nonetheless, off we went to the Race. When got to our parking lot, we set out some folding chairs, started drinking Electric Lemonade and beer, and ate chicken and hot dogs while we waited to see how the weather would treat us.

The Race was scheduled to start at 12:40, but we went in at 11:00 to watch the pre-race festivities. They had a bunch of old racecars parade around the track, including a car driven by Mario Andretti, who was celebrating the 50th anniversary of his only Indy 500 win. There were many other presentations that ended with the introduction of the 33 drivers.

When the start time was getting close, the track announcer asked all the armed services veterans to stand and receive a round of applause. Then the announcer asked the crowd to stand in silence while Taps was played. Over 300,000 fans were perfectly silent. Most had their hats off and their hands over their hearts. It was so moving a moment that tears came to the eyes of many, including me.

When Taps was completed, we were asked to remain standing while God Bless America and America the Beautiful were sung. Then, finally, the Star-Spangled Banner. Most fans continued to remain silent during all of this. Some sang along to the National Anthem.

A fly-over of jets was timed to streak over the Speedway at the end of the Anthem, and that brought a roar from the crowd. One of the jets came back after the fly-over and circled the interior of the Speedway at low altitude, then darted strait up and kept going until it was out of sight. The fans went nuts.

The Race started a few minutes later, and it was run without any rain.

* * *

During recent times, an open expression of patriotism sometimes is looked upon as a misguided sentiment that harkens back to a time when Americans falsely believed our country was exceptional. Our last President told us that he believed in American exceptionalism in the same way that the French or Greeks believe in French or Greek exceptionalism.

Our current President tells us he wants to Make America Great Again. His opponents tell us America never was all that great. Academics tell us that America is infected by an inherent original sin arising out of the racism of our founding fathers, all of whom were white men. Millionaire athletes tell us that protesting the singing of the National Anthem before sporting events is patriotic. Politicians from Washington D.C. patronize Americans in the fly-over country between the east and west coasts as ignorant deplorables clinging to their guns and bibles. All these attitudes are bolstered by the mainstream media.

The 75th anniversary of the Normandy Invasion is an especially appropriate time to consider these attitudes, and the long-term outcome is far from certain.

It's been so long since World War II that remembrances of it have faded. Of the 16 million Americans in the U.S. armed forces during World War II, only about 400,000 survive, and over 400 of them die each day. There are ever dwindling numbers people who personally knew men like Chester Dzialo, so first-hand accounts of that war increasingly are unavailable to young men and women.

High schools and colleges do not teach much about World War II. Instead, most of what students are taught about our heritage comes from academics who protested against America's patriotic traditions during the Vietnam era. Our media largely comes from and promotes the same anti-American Vietnam era attitudes. In the face of all this, it's hard not to wonder whether today's youth would defend our country from outside attack in the same way that The Greatest Generation rose to the occasion during World War II.

But there is much about which to be optimistic. Today, Vietnam veterans receive the respect that they earned but were denied when they served our country. Productions like *Band of Brothers* and institutions like the D-Day Museum in New Orleans preserve a record of the brave Americans who served in World War II, and at the same time promote the American exceptionalism that was assumed to exist just a couple of generations ago.

Unlike during the Vietnam era, we now have an all-volunteer military. It is the best equipped and best trained military in the world. Civilians who encounter soldiers now routinely thank them for their service.

Perhaps most encouraging is the love of country emanating from Middle America. If you want to experience a genuine pride in America, go to the Indianapolis 500. Go to any sporting event, concert or county fair in the Heartland and you will have the same experience I had at this year's Race. Witness the decline in NFL attendance and TV ratings when millionaire athletes insulted their fans by taking a knee during the National Anthem.

Screw the elites who disparage our country. The United States of America is the greatest country in the history of the world, and we live in the best time in history to live here. The 75th anniversary of D-day is a perfect time to thank all who served to keep us free.

So, to our veterans, thank you and God Bless America.

Politically Incorrect Stories

These stories are pretty benign for people of my generation. But in today's "Cancel Culture," they might cause the Snowflake lefties who want to censor anything with which they disagree to scamper to their safe spaces. I think these stories are just plain fun and I hope you'll enjoy them.

Sam Allen: A Half Million Miles of Road Trips

The Oxford Five:
I was in jail with these guys.

Me the year I masterminded the Great Ole Miss Streak

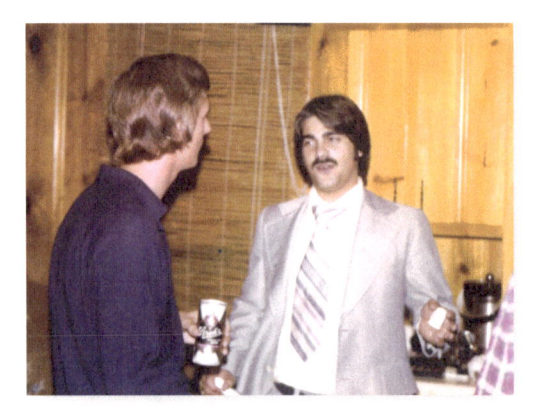

The wheel man. Known as "Lefty" because his left nut was as big as a softball.

James Logan Collier was one of the instigators.

Aimless Bill was along for the thrill.

Tommy "Baby Huey" Cox:
The getaway driver.

Politically Incorrect Stories

This is the story of my "streak" down Sorority Row at Ole Miss in 1974.

Five Hard Men

It was a crisp North Mississippi Sunday night in 1974. It should have been a sleepy time in a sleepy town. But at 10:30 five hard men climbed into cars to get to the Target Zone that in a few minutes later would be the site of a caper so audacious that it would change the lives of thousands of women and capture national attention.

The Ringleader was Sam Allen. Before this Caper, he was known as "Sambo". After the Caper he became known as "Insane Sam".

The Wheel man was Dave "Lefty" Tranberg, who got that name because his left nut was the size of a softball. "Aimless" Bill Amos and Jamie "James Logan" Collier were providing support.

As Lefty pulled into the street, Burgess "Tommy" Cox cruised to the other end of the Target Zone in his silver Ford Maverick. He drove just fast enough not to get stopped for speeding, but not so slow as to draw the attention of the local police. He was the getaway driver, and everything depended on him. If he was not exactly where he was supposed to be at exactly the right time, everyone likely be in jail within the hour.

It wasn't a long drive to the Target Zone. The gang had traveled less than a mile. Lefty went around one final corner and stopped. Without a word, Sam put on a ski mask, opened the car door and bolted. Lefty and the others were on their own. Insane Sam was confident because he would cause enough of a diversion that Lefty, Aimless Bill and James Logan would be able to slip away in the confusion.

* * *

Three hours earlier I had been in the Alpha Tau Omega Fraternity House at Ole Miss studying for an exam I had in Comparative Religions the next morning. That was curious in itself because there usually wasn't much studying at the ATO House. Back then, the ATO's were like *Animal House*, except Delta's in the movie were a lot more studious than the Ole Miss ATO's. I joined ATO in the fall of 1973 in a pledge class of 44 freshmen. To get initiated into the fraternity, the University required a grade point average of 2.0. My pledge class's cumulative grade point average was 1.6, with only 21 of the 44 of us achieving the required 2.0. There were several "Buckshots": 0.0. I brought our average up with a GPA of 4.0.

The spring of 1974 was when the "Streaking" craze peaked. As much beer as we drank at Ole Miss, it was a pretty conservative place, and there had been no streaking on our campus. While I was studying, a fraternity brother came into my room with a rumor that someone was going to streak down Sorority Row at 9:00. A group of us decided to go to watch.

When we got there, thousands of sorority girls lined the road. The campus police were everywhere. It was evident no one was going to streak so we went back to the fraternity house.

A couple of hours later we decided to go back to Sorority Row to see if anything had changed. There still were thousands of people assembled, but the police seemingly had disappeared. We hung around a while without seeing streaker, and on impulse I said I'd do it.

We went back to the fraternity house and from somewhere a wool knit ski mask was produced. Tommy Cox headed toward the end of Sorority Row to be my getaway driver, and Lefty, Jamie, Bill and I piled into Lefty's car to head to the top of Sorority Row.

* * *

When I hopped out of Lefty's car I hauled ass. The course was almost half a mile long, but it was downhill all the way. I did not know it at the time, but as soon as I got out of the car police sprang from various hiding places and chased me all the way down Sorority Row with guns drawn. What I remember most was a mass of people cheering and hundreds of flash bulbs going off.

Tommy was exactly where he was supposed to be. I jumped into the Maverick, and he took off. He had brought a sweat suit along so I could put clothes on quickly, and I ditched the ski mask. Tommy took a hard-right off Sorority Row onto Jackson Avenue, and a few hundred yards later turned around and headed slowly back toward campus. Police cars with lights blazing and sirens screaming raced past us going the opposite direction, and we knew we had gotten away.

It was only a five-minute ride back to the fraternity house. When we got there, about 20 of our fraternity brothers were on the front lawn wearing nothing but their underwear. John Cranfield, greeted us.

Cran was a typical ATO. He believed any grade above a 2.0 was wasted effort. Cran also was an instigator. He seemed to be involved in everything but never got caught for anything.

Cran said "They got Tranberg. He got away, but he drove back to the scene of the crime and the police picked him up".

Tommy and I knew Lefty would break under the police questioning. A couple of years previously he had taken a rap for stealing steaks. Cran had told Lefty that if he was going to steal some steaks he should steal one for him too. Lefty was apprehended leaving Kroger's with two tenderloins down his pants by his tender loins. It must have been a tight fit with two steaks and a softball sized nut in there. With this past criminal record, Lefty was facing the Death Penalty for being the wheel man for a Mississippi streaker.

Tommy and I opened a couple beers and waited for the police to come.

When they arrived, were put into a brand-new paddy wagon. The police told us we were the first prisoners to ride in it. They took us to the Lafayette County Jail. We were fingerprinted, and when they took our mug shots, the police photographer said, "Make a mean face for the camera". We did, and Tommy said, "What are you going to do Kojak, give us the chair?"

The police didn't seem to find much humor in what we had done, but I hoped that if we were polite they would let us go with a warning. It didn't work out that way. The next thing we knew, we were in Cell Number 2 with Lefty, Jamie and Aimless Bill. I had been charged with indecent exposure, and the rest of the crew was charged with the unlikely crime of aiding and abetting indecent exposure.

The next morning, they brought us Egg McMuffin's from McDonald's for breakfast, and soon after that Dr. Bela Chain, an ATO in the Ole Miss administrative offices, bailed us out. We made national news when Walter Cronkite reported that the streaking craze had hit Ole Miss, where five students had been arrested for streaking the previous night. Fortunately, he didn't name us.

The five of us met with some influential ATO alumnae from Oxford, and they assured us that they could get the charges dropped. That seemed a likely outcome when a few days later hundreds of Ole Miss students had a mass streak with a police escort.

About a week after my streak I was having lunch at the fraternity house, and someone told me my father was on the hall telephone. I knew that could not be good. My father never called me while I was at school. I picked up the receiver and with my best perky voice said, "Hey Dad!"

He asked, "What the hell have you been up to down there?"

"Just studying hard, Dad! Really hitting the books!"

"Don't give me that crap, have you been in jail?"

I had to fess up and I told him the story. But I wondered how he found out about my streak.

Here's what happened: Unknown to my father or me, my father's law partner in Connecticut, Chester Dzialo, was married to a woman whose sister was married to a history professor from Ole Miss. The professor read about my streak in the student body newspaper, recognized my name, and ratted me out. I later made A's in his Roman History and Greek History classes. I also got him back by dating his daughter. I don't think he liked that too much.

The "Ole Miss Five" appeared in Lafayette County District Court No. 4 before Judge Harry Turpin. The fix was supposed to be in. We were going to plead guilty to disorderly conduct and be let off for time served and without a fine. But the Judge trick-fucked us and fined each of us $50. That was a lot of money in those days. My whole monthly budget was $200, comprised of $106 to live and eat at the fraternity house, and $94 for other expenses. I got a construction job to pay my fines.

Looking back, I think my mother was pretty upset, but deep down, my father thought "That's my boy"! He was making a half-hearted effort to play the Bad Cop.

My father used to write me letters that were so funny I would post them on fraternity house bulletin board. After I'd been convicted of disorderly conduct and got a construction job to pay my fines, he wrote me a letter, which in pertinent part, said:

> "Your mother and I would like you to remember that you are in college for purpose. Obtaining a construction job to earn the funds necessary to pay fines levied for unlawful deeds is not in accordance with that purpose. Hitherto, your mother and I have not heard of any our friends children being arrested for studying in their spare time."

The rest of the letter made clear that I damn well better come home with all A's at the end of the semester. I brought home the demanded A's, but the story did not end there.

After graduating from Ole Miss I wound up working construction, tending bar and doing the other kinds of things that young men do between graduating from college and figuring out what they are going to do with their lives. For me, one of those things was getting married to a Tri Delta girl who had witnessed the streak three years before I met her. I wound up going to Washington and Lee Law School, where I graduated in 1982. After law school I moved to New York to practice law at Brown, Wood, Ivey, Mitchell & Petty in the World Trade Center.

I passed the Bar Exam and submitted the lengthy application required for admittance. One of the questions was whether I ever been arrested. I couldn't lie, and I didn't even try to fudge the facts. However, I was enough of a lawyer even then to say I had been arrested for streaking rather than indecent exposure.

A few months after submitting my Application, I received a letter from the New York Bar informing me that I was to appear before the

Bar's Character and Fitness Committee to determine whether my illicit past would be an impediment to my admission to the New York Bar.

The interview was held in the offices of a Midtown law firm the name of which I now forget. I showed up at the appointed time and was escorted into a conference room to meet with the Character and Fitness Committee, which consisted of one anciently old guy. I took a seat while the Inquisitor shuffled through some papers for a minute or so without speaking to me. Then he looked me without even a twinkle in his eyes, said "Tell me in your own words about this streaking incident."

I told him the story. He didn't seem to find any humor in it. He asked, "Was it fun?"

I told him that it was. When he didn't smile, I interjected that the streaking part was fun but the going to jail part wasn't. He asked whether I planned on doing it again. I pointed out that the streak had occurred eight years previously when I was 19 years old, and that my record had been clean since then. I promised that I wouldn't streak again.

He gave me a long stern look, and finally said, "Well Mr. Allen, I don't suppose there's any reason that you should be denied admission to the Bar of the State of New York."

I stood up, said thank you, shook his hand, and commenced my storied career as a high-powered corporate finance lawyer.

Endnote: *About a year and a half ago I was at an Ole Miss football game with all the guys who went to jail with me for participating in the streak. I filmed interviews with everybody and turned it into a video that's posted on my YouTube channel, Route 66 Party Guide. It's my favorite video on the channel, and I think you'll find it hilarious. If you want to watch the Video, open* bit.ly/3kYtMIS *in your browser.*

If the Cancel Culture Nazi's ever come after me, it might be because of this story and the video version of it that is posted on my YouTube channel, Route 66 Party Guide.

10 Things You Don't Do in a Biker Bar

Over the last couple of days I've been riding through Oklahoma, and yesterday I saw something pretty frightening. In fact, I saw it twice.

I had just been by the Blue Whale in Catoosa and was headed toward Tulsa when I saw a big burly guy with a beard riding on the back of some other guy's motorcycle. That's called riding "Bitch," and that's something guys don't do. A little later on I was going through Oklahoma City, and I saw a guy riding Bitch on the back of a chick's bike. That's something I'd never seen.

I couldn't figure out which was worse. It would be one thing if these were kids, but they looked to be well into their 20s. It also would be different if scooters were involved, but these were Harley-Davidsons. Maybe it would be OK if there was some kind of emergency that could be resolved only through the back seat solution. But these guys had grins and looked to be having a big time. Maybe this was some kind of transgender thing and everyone was so good at being transgender I couldn't tell they were transgender.

I can sort of understand why a guy would get on the back of a chick's bike, as long as it involved a lot of alcohol and a chance for some biker chick sex.

The implications of all this are troublesome. I have tried to put it out of my mind, but I haven't had any luck with that. After much thought, I've decided the only way to cleanse my memory of those images is to confront them head on and to turn the negative into a positive. So, as a public service to guys in Oklahoma and elsewhere, here are 10 things guys should not do in the biker world. Pay attention; it might save your life.

10. Don't go to a biker bar and sit on another guy's bike.
9. Don't go to a biker bar and order a Daiquiri.
8. Don't go up to a Hells Angel and try to take his picture.
7. Don't go to a biker bar and start hitting on women you don't know.
6. Don't go up to a Hells Angel and say "That's a cool vest. Where can I get one?"
5. Don't tell a bunch of bikers that smoking isn't allowed in the bar you are in.
4. Don't go to a bar with a couple of friends and ask a biker "Do you mind if we dance with your dates?"
3. Don't go up to a biker chick who's got a tattoo that says, "Property of Killer Joe" and say, "Show me your tits."
2. Don't go up to a biker and ask him who he likes better: Sean Hannity or Bill O'Reilly.
1. **Don't ride bitch!**

Endnote: *For reasons I don't quite fathom, the video about 10 things you don't do in a biker bar has had more views than any other video I have posted on my YouTube Channel, Route 66 Party Guide. To see the video, open* bit.ly/3l08cii *in your browser.*

That video is so popular I'm going to shoot a new one called "10 More Things you don't do in a Biker Bar." I've never published this as a blog, so you are going to be the first to have the benefit of this advice.

10. Don't go into a biker bar and play a bunch of songs on the juke box by K C and the Sunshine Band.
9. Don't go into a biker bat wearing a cardigan sweater.
8. Don't go into a biker bar and tell everybody that you love bikers and that Born to be Wild is your favorite song.
7. Don't go into a biker bar and tell everyone the pronouns you identify with.

6. *Don't go into a biker bar where everyone is watching an MMA fight on TV and ask if you can change it to golf.*
5. *Don't go into a biker bar and offer to teach everyone how to line dance.*
4. *Don't go into a biker bar and ask where the minivan parking is.*
3. *Don't go into a biker bar and tell everyone you are a lesbian biker trapped in a man's body and you are dating your mother's girlfriend.*
2. *Don't go into a biker bar and say "My girlfriend has never been on a motorcycle. Will one of you guys give her a ride?*
1. **Don't ride bitch!**

People tell me I have food phobias. I disagree. I think that when you read this story you'll admit you feel the same way about most of these attitudes.

Eat Me!

One of the best things about city living is the plethora of great restaurants. It's hard for bad restaurants to survive in cities because there are so many good ones from which to choose. That's not the case in rural America. You just have to take what you can find. I was in Moriarty, New Mexico the other night and things were so grim I had to dine at a 7/11 convenience store. I had a bottle of water and a bag of almonds for dinner.

Sure, many small towns have good places to eat, especially where regional specialties are involved, like Mexican food in Texas or steaks in Nebraska. But those are the exceptions. Here are some guidelines for eating on the road and determining what food to eat in general.

First of all, never eat at a restaurant that claims to have "Kountry Kookin.'" A place with "Down Home Kountry Kookin'" probably is worse. They all specialize in meat loaf with greasy mushroom gravy and all day breakfast. They serve vegetables that are hours, maybe days, over cooked.

If liver and onions are on the menu go somewhere else or order something that never touches the grill. Otherwise, the liver juices might seep into your pancakes. Not only do you not want liver juice on your pancakes, you shouldn't eat liver at all.

You should avoid ordering a Cup "O" Soup or any other hyphenated food. That's not a universal restriction, but there are plenty of foods that should be avoided dogmatically.

The first is the digestive or sex organs of any animal. Thus the taboo on liver mentioned above. Liver produces bile. I'm not eating any bile. Kidneys basically are piss strainers, and we all know what tripe carries.

Out west some people eat Rocky Mountain Oysters. Never eat them. If your date eats them don't kiss her or him for the earlier to expire of (i) the documented completion of the gargling of a large bottle of original Listerine and the use of an entire roll of floss; (ii) the completion of the next professionally administered teeth cleaning and the execution and delivery of a certificate from the dentist, sworn under penalty of perjury, that there is no remaining debris; and (iii) one year from the date the Oysters were eaten.

Never eat the meat of curly haired animals. Nappy haired is OK.

Don't eat fish. Bad fish tastes "fishy." I've never had a steak that was too beefy.

Never eat animals that have tentacles or suction cups.

Never eat anything that doesn't have any legs, except clams, oysters (of the marine variety) and muscles, and then only eat them if they are cooked.

No lizards.

Don't eat things that are supposed to be tasty if prepared properly but are poisonous if not prepared properly.

Don't eat yellow sauces unless they are made of cheese.

Never eat ketchup before noon. Some people have asked me about that rule and hamburgers at an early lunch. That's an easy one. Never eat lunch before noon.

Never eat dinner before dark, except in the case of summer cookouts.

Don't eat anything green and soft. Soft green food either is over cooked vegetables or has avocado in it. Both of these should be avoided.

Don't eat any vegetables from countries with high incidents of leprosy or vegetables that reproduce from spores.

Except for carrots, corn, onions and peppers, do not eat vegetables that are not green.

Don't eat funny looking vegetables. These include but are not limited to cauliflower, eggplant, turnips, rhubarb, artichokes, hearts of palm (what are they?) and Brussels sprouts.

Don't eat gourds.

Asparagus is especially insidious. A person seeing asparagus for the first time likely would wonder how to put the batteries in.

Never eat breads or deserts made from vegetables.

Fruits identified with foreign countries should not be eaten. So, mangos, guavas, papayas, figs, pomegranates and dates are out. Regular fruits that happen to be grown in a foreign country are OK. So, bananas and pineapples are in.

Speaking of fruits, never eat overly fuzzy ones. Peaches are OK because the fuzz is not intrusive. Kiwis are fine because you cut the fuzz off before eating them. Apricots are not OK because they are like a mouthful of fuzz. There is only one mouth full of fuzz kind of thing that can be eaten, and an apricot isn't it.

Don't eat fruit that must be peeled to eat but has baggy skin. So, oranges and bananas are OK because they have tight skins. Tangerines are out.

There are some fruits that are funny looking and are of from uncertain origin. There is a thing called a star fruit. I'm not that adventurous.

Never eat Chinese food in a town with less than 500,000 people.

Never eat mayonnaise except in chicken salad or pasta salad, and then use only Hellman's.

Cole slaw is out. In fact, never allow Cole slaw on your plate. The juice from the slaw will migrate onto your other food, like your fries or hamburger roll, and it's almost impossible to amputate the affected area completely.

Because of this rule I get accused of not liking my various foods on a plate touching each other. That's not true. I don't mind foods I like touching each other; I just don't want things I do like being contaminated by things I don't like.

Hot dogs are a delicate matter. Try to get Nathan's or Hebrew National. For sure don't eat some brand that is not all beef. They taste like Spam (for that matter, never eat Spam). I realize that the beef in an all-beef hot dog does not from good places, but this is a don't ask-don't tell situation.

All hot dogs should be eaten with regular mustard. Yellow or spicy is fine but avoid fancy mustard. Grey Poupon on a hot dog does not work.

Although "mustard only" is preferable, a maximum of one additional topping is acceptable. So, you can have mustard and sauerkraut, mustard and onions or mustard and pickled relish (the best is Claussen), but you can't have mustard, sauerkraut and relish.

Never, under any circumstances, put ketchup on a hot dog. In Texas, some people put mayonnaise on a hot dog. That is revolting on its face separately from the general prohibition of mayonnaise.

Eating hot dogs among some groups can be a problem. I eat my hot dogs in the traditional way, but I know some homophobes in Houston who are so afraid of being branded as gay that they eat their hot dogs like corn on the cob.

There is more flexibility on hamburgers, but there are a few guidelines. Always use round hamburger rolls. Grilled rye bread is OK, but only in the case of a "patty melt", which has grilled onions and Swiss cheese. If the onions are not grilled or any other type of cheese is used, go back to the round roll. It's not a patty melt. Plus, always remember: No mayonnaise.

Then there are foods with "live cultures." First of all, I'm not sure I want cultures at all, but if I have to eat cultures I want mine dead. Eating live ones is like eating something from a petre dish. Lots of these live culture foods seem to be things that have gone bad, like sour cream. Never eat it. I'm not sure if cottage cheese has the same principle, but I'm pretty sure it's curdled milk. It doesn't matter. Cottage cheese comes under the general "funny looking" ban.

I like pudding and I like regular fruits, and yogurt is sort of like fruit pudding. So, I really tried to like yogurt, but I've never been able to get over the thought of those cultures squiggling around.

A troubling situation can arise when foods to be avoided are served when you are someone's guest. On the one hand, you don't want to be rude. On the other hand, you don't want to eat what's been served up. The perfect resolution is to claim you are allergic to the stuff you don't want to eat.

This is a partial list, but if you follow these rules you ought to be able to navigate through most situations.

Some people tell me that these are odd dietary restrictions; *however*, I've found that many people agree with them without letting on. Kind of like saying you hate Donald Trump when you know you are going to vote for him in the secrecy of the voting booth.

Eat Me! Bonus

THE FEEDBACK I RECEIVED regarding my guides to gastronomic righteousness confirmed that my eating rules are close to being metaphysical truths. Still, some of the commentary compels me to revise and expand upon these matters.

The exclusive exceptions against eating animals with more than four legs are lobsters, crabs and crawfish.

Ordinarily, okra would come under the prohibition against eating funny looking vegetables; *however*, okra is OK in gumbo in the sense that you can still eat the gumbo as long as you don't eat the okra itself.

Never eat hummus. The problem is the difference between humus and hummus. Humus is the part of soil formed by leaves and other plants decomposed by soil microorganisms. On the other hand, hummus is an Egyptian food made from mashed chickpeas. The later sounds too much like the former. If that isn't enough, you shouldn't eat Egyptian food. Most of it comes from curly rather than nappy haired animals.

Don't eat cold potatoes in any form.

Don't eat pate.

Don't eat tongue. It makes you think your food is tasting you back.

Don't allow Mexican food in your car.

Drink Me!

My last blog posting chronicled common sense rules for identifying the best foods to eat and foods that most right thinking people avoid. This is a follow up article focusing on the consumption of alcoholic beverages. While the food related rules should be followed dogmatically, the drinking rules are more in the nature of guidelines that are malleable depending on the context.

The whole point of drinking is to have a good time. Always sit at the bar. There is no action at a table.

You should drink what makes you happy. There are some guidelines, but even they may be taken in context. For instance, if you are in a cowboy bar in Ingomar, Montana, and a hot chick offers to buy you a shooter, you should not order a Tequila Rose. Order real tequila. Folks out west, including the women, don't drink pussy shooters.

On the other hand, if you are in a bar in New Orleans and a hot chick offers to buy you a drink, you can order as flamboyantly as you like. Just be sure the chick is not some dude who is identifying as a woman that day.

There are too many great shooters to list. The worst shooter ever is the Itchy and Scratchy: Half tequila and half 151 proof rum. The Harley Oil also is bad: Half Jeager and half Jack Daniels.

I don't worry about mixing different kinds of booze. Some people claim that mixing alcohols gives them a hangover. Their stories usually go something like this: I met this chick at a sports bar one Sunday afternoon while I was watching football. She was great and we drank a bunch of beer. Then we decided to go to dinner, and I had a few Martini's at the bar before we got seated. We had a couple of bottles of wine with dinner then had some Gran Marnier's after dinner. I drove her home and she invited me in for a night cap. I wound up staying the night and had a fantastic time, but I was really hung over the next morning, so I don't mix my alcohol anymore.

Give me a break. You think it might have been the volume rather than the mixture that caused the problem?

I don't go brown until after sundown. I usually start off with a beer, sometimes two. Then I go to white wine. I like the pinot grigio. After wine I graduate to Tanqueray and tonic. I can have as much of any of those beverages as I like, but no whiskey until after dark. That can be a problem in the summer because the days are so much longer. So sometimes I bend this rule a bit and go brown at dusk.

Never drink before noon except at tailgate parties for football games.

Never use those small hollow swizzle sticks like straws. For that matter, don't use straws while drinking except for rum based drinks in New Orleans, South Florida or on any beach or island (other than Manhattan).

Glassware is important. The best glass is a 10 oz. highball glass. Unfortunately, hardly any bars use them anymore. The most common glasses in use are those short octagonal glasses that bartenders can stack up. They are horrible. I leave my own glassware in bars that use them. Here are a few other glassware tips:

Don't drink any mixed drink from a glass that can be stacked up.

Don't drink anything except wine or a martini from a stemmed glass.

Don't drink beer out of a glass with a brown bottom.

Never buy Bourbon made outside of Bourbon County Kentucky.

Don't drink Jack Daniels after turning 19 years old or after your freshman year in college, whichever comes first.

Never buy Scotch made outside of Scotland.

Never buy alcohol that comes in a plastic bottle.

Never buy alcohol, other than beer, that is manufactured in New Orleans.

Don't buy beer that comes in a bottle of more than 32 ounces or that is made out of water from the Latrobe River.

Never drink Ripple, Champale, Boone's Farm wine of any flavor, Mad Dog 20-20 or malt liquor. Wine coolers are Ok during the summer months.

Don't drink Champaign that comes in a bottle with a plastic cork.

Don't sip Champaign. It's best when guzzled. I like drinking it out of a frosted beer mug. Mimosas also should be guzzled. Make them strong. The orange juice should be added with an eyedropper.

My Dear Old Dad taught me not to put soft drinks in whiskey. He said, "Sonny boy, a man puts only one of two things in his whiskey: ice or more whiskey." That advice had a certain irony to it since he was drinking a whiskey sour at the time. I like to drink about four fingers of Bourbon with lots of ice and a splash of club soda. That gives me some bubbles without changing the taste of the booze. Real whiskey purists don't condone the ice or the club soda. That's especially true of Scotch drinkers.

If you are drunk in a hotel room and go to a vending machine in the middle of the night to get a Coca Cola, be sure to put some clothes on. Also be sure to bring the key to your room. Write the room number on your hand to be sure you can find your way back.

Any article about drinking alcohol should emphasize the dangers of alcohol abuse and safety matters. Safety for yourself and those with whom you may come in contact is of paramount importance. Everybody knows that drinking and driving can be criminal, but it's also irresponsible to put yourself, your passengers and others on the road in jeopardy. If you are drunk, don't drive. Call Uber and get home safely. However, if you find yourself behind the wheel while impaired, you should drive home at the fastest possible speed. Following this simple safety rule shortens the time you are on the road, thus shortening the period during which you might harm yourself or others.

If a policeman pulls you over:

Don't call him Kojak or Deputy Fife.

Don't ask him if he knows any horny chicks you can bond out of jail.

If he gives you a field sobriety test don't say "Shit, man, I couldn't do this if I was sober!"

If you are feeling sick while taking the test, try not to throw up, and if you do throw up, don't do it on the officer's shoe.

Don't ask him where to find an after-hours bar.

If he arrests you, call a lawyer not your mother.

If you are in a cell, when they bring around the bologna sandwiches, don't ask if they have any Grey Poupon.

Remember these are guidelines and not rules. To be sure you use your best judgment on how they apply to you, pop a top or cork, or if it's after sundown down a couple of strong ones, and consider the guidelines with the benefit of a mellow glow.

Sam Allen Route 66 Projects

In addition to this collection of Blogs, I recently published the Third Edition of *The Route 66 Party Guide*. I also have a website called route66mc.com and other social media, as well as a YouTube channel called *Route 66 Party Guide* that has nearly 100 posted videos. Most recently, I started a Roku TV Channel called *Route 66 Party Guide*.

The Route 66 Party Guide: The Book

I recently published an all new Third Edition of my book, *The Route 66 Party Guide*. It has over 100 more photographs than the previous edition, and the photos are larger and with higher resolution. Everything has been updated, so all the information is current.

A full color version is available on Kindle as an e-book, and a full color hard copy version is available on my website, *route66mc.com*.

Route66mc.com and Other Social Media

Route66mc.com

Route66mc.com is one of the most unique and entertaining Route 66 websites. It has:

- A separate web page for each Route 66 town, with photos, local history and attractions.

- 🛡 Most of the web pages have short videos created from the videos posted on my YouTube channel, *Route 66 Party Guide*, so you can view entertaining videos as you use *route66mc.com* to navigate Route 66.
- 🛡 Turn by turn directions between any two Route 66 Towns.
- 🛡 Information about all of the classic Route 66 Roadside Attractions, plus many Attractions not found on other web sites, like Rex the Freeze Dried Dog.
- 🛡 Suggested bars, restaurants, motels, motor courts, restaurants and drive-ins.
- 🛡 Personal stories about my adventures on Route 66, like the time I locked myself out of my hotel room, naked, without my room key and not remembering my room number.
- 🛡 Access to the Blogs I have published about Route 66 and other adventures I've has riding America's roads on a motorcycle.

Other Social Media

- 🛡 Facebook/Route66mc.com
- 🛡 Instagram@PartyGuideRoute66
- 🛡 Twitter@PartyGuideRoute66

Route 66 Party Guide: The YouTube Channel

My YouTube channel is called *Route 66 Party Guide*. It is the most unique and informative channel on YouTube about Route 66. There are nearly 100 videos posted in seven Playlists.

The Playlists

Route 66 in 10 Days

This Playlist has 27 videos that will guide you from Chicago to LA on Route 66 in 10 days. I know it can be done because I've done it myself on a motorcycle in 8½ days.

These videos are among the most informative videos about Route 66 you'll find on YouTube. But they also are hilarious! Check out Insane Sam's Hit Parade below.

Insane Sam's Hit Parade

Open the links below in your browser to see videos of song's I wrote about famous sights along Route 66. Sometimes I dress up in costumes, like when I sing:

- The Corn Dog Rap bit.ly/41lToKB
- The T-Bone Sizzle bit.ly/41Mc7Vr
- Dinosaur Breath bit.ly/3Jpf5bD
- White Rabbit bit.ly/3wFgHXk
- The Crazy Chicken Saloon Tune bit.ly/3DjRjtZ

Route 66 History

Open the links below for videos about:

- A Brief History of Route 66 . . . . bit.ly/3ZpybDT
- Bonnie and Clyde on Route 66 . . . . bit.ly/3kWe9BJ
- The Coral Court Caper Part 1 . . . . bit.ly/3YFjb3H
- The Kidnapping of Bobby Greenlease and the Coral Court bit.ly/3mwEjf7
- Exploring La Bajada Hill bit.ly/41MhYKp

Route 66 Top 10s

These videos tell you about my Top 10 favorite:

- Route 66 Motorcycle Rides;
- Towns;

- 🛣 Roadside Attractions;
- 🛣 Hotels;
- 🛣 Motor Courts;
- 🛣 Bars;
- 🛣 Restaurants; and
- 🛣 Drive-Ins.

Route 66 Road Trip Clips

Open the links below to see short clips I filmed along the way while exploring Route 66. They include visits to:

- 🛣 **Henry's Drive** in, Cicero, IL bit.ly/3Rh5q9g
- 🛣 **Dick's on 66**, Joliette, IL bit.ly/3XMiLZB
- 🛣 **Rex the Freeze Dried Dog**, Wilmington, IL . bit.ly/3HErsj1
- 🛣 **Two Cell Jail**, Gardner, IL bit.ly/3wDgjlS
- 🛣 **Wild Bill Hickok Shoot Out**, Springfield, IL   bit.ly/3HhakhU
- 🛣 **Lucille's Roadhouse**, Weatherford, OK bit.ly/3LiDfWz

Roads Less Traveled

These videos are about places that are close to my heart. Open the links below for a couple of my favorites:

- 🛣 **Memory Lane**, Lexington, IL bit.ly/3Jfn2zl
- 🛣 **Over the Rainbow**, Yellowstone, Wyoming . . bit.ly/4lObw5A
- 🛣 **Ain't no Memories in First Class**,
  Red Oak II, Missouri bit.ly/3lRuHD3

Politically Incorrect Videos

These videos are exactly what they sound like. Here are a couple that might get me canceled.

- 10 Things You Don't Do in a Biker Bar bit.ly/3I08cii
- **Five Hard Men** bit.ly/3kYtMIS
- **Eat Me** bit.ly/3ITGYqC
- **J S Cranfield Big Easy Tequila** bit.ly/3ZOgXjn
- **God Bless America!** bit.ly/3IVy7Vb

About the Author

There were hints that Sam Allen was twisted when he was arrested as the first Streaker at Ole Miss.

Despite his early legal transgressions, Sam's criminal record ultimately was expunged, and he graduated from law school. He has been a lawyer for 40 years, first practicing at a major New York City law firm and later as a partner in the corporate finance section of a Houston, Texas firm. His practice focuses on corporate finance, and he has been named as a Texas Super Lawyer in that field. Sam taught Securities Regulation at the University of Houston Law School. He has written many articles on legal issues, most recently with respect to cryptocurrencies for the Gonzaga University Law School Crypto After Dark seminar. He has been in private practice since 2011.

While practicing law in New York, Sam boxed in Madison Square Garden and published an article about the experience in New York Magazine. After that, he was featured in People Magazine and on NBC Nightly News as New York's boxing lawyer.

Sam had been riding up and down Route 66 for years but always explored only small sections of the Mother Road on any particular trip. When he entered private law practice in 2011, he took his first trip on Route 66 from Chicago to Los Angeles.

While on that trip Sam decided to take notes to write some articles about the experience. That effort soon became a project to create his own Route 66 website, and *route66mc.com* was launched in 2013. In 2014 he published *The Route 66 Motorcycle Party Guide*, and in 2023 he published the third edition of that book.

Sam produced *Kicks on Route 66*, which is a pilot TV show about riding motorcycles on Route 66.

He started the *Route 66 Party Guide* YouTube channel in 2021, and he has posted 95 videos on that channel so far.

In 2002, Sam founded the Deacons of Deadwood Motorcycle Club. The Deacons started with 13 businessmen, and now has about 80 members. The Club has donated nearly $4,000,000 to charities benefiting children in the Houston area.